YOU ONLY HAVE TO DIE

YOU ONLY HAVE TO DIE

*LEADING YOUR CONGREGATION TO
NEW LIFE*

JAMES A. HARNISH

Abingdon Press / Nashville

YOU ONLY HAVE TO DIE:
LEADING YOUR CONGREGATION TO NEW LIFE

Copyright © 2004 by Abingdon Press

This book is printed on recycled, acid-free elemental-chlorine free paper.

Library of Congress Cataloging-in-Publication Data

Harnish, James A.
   You only have to die : leading your congregation to new life / James A. Harnish.
      p. cm.
   ISBN 0-687-06688-3 (alk. paper)
   1. Church renewal. 2. Church growth. 3. Mission of the church. I. Title.

BV652.25.H37 2004
253—dc22

2003021506

ISBN 13: 978-0-687-06688-9

09 10 11 12 13 – 10 9 8 7

MANUFACTURED IN THE UNITED STATES OF AMERICA

Give me an undivided heart to revere your name.

—Psalm 86:11

CONTENTS

THOSE FOR WHOM THIS BOOK IS WRITTEN

This book is for real people whose faces I hold in my imagination as I write . . .

. . . the young pastor who is struggling to lead a long-established congregation that seems to resist the very changes that might give it hope for the future.

. . . the 20-something career woman who is searching for a congregation that values the spiritual traditions in which she was raised but is passionately committed to communicating the gospel to her friends, none of whom share her Christian history.

. . . the retired couple who want their church to be as effective in reaching young couples today as it was when they arrived just after World War II.

. . . the clergy couple who are guiding a very diverse congregation in finding a common center for its ministry after the retirement of a beloved pastor who held the congregation together for two decades by the warmth of his personality and pastoral care.

. . . the businessman who would like to see his congregation function with the clarity of purpose that he sees in some of the best corporations.

. . . the retired bishop who prays that historically vibrant but now-declining congregations in his area will discover new vitality for the future.

. . . the clergy and lay leaders who have been just far enough ahead of me on this journey to show me the next step to take.

. . . the soul-friend who gave me the CD of Steven Curtis Chapman singing, "For the Sake of the Call" and for people around the world who prayed for the healing of my heart.

. . . and, most of all, for the people of Hyde Park United Methodist Church in Tampa, Florida, with whom I share the continuing surprise of all that God is doing among us!

Soli Deo Gloria!

CHAPTER 1
All the Way to the Heart

"The LORD does not see as mortals see; they look on the outward appearance, but the LORD looks on the heart." —1 Samuel 16:7

If you forget everything else you read in this book, I hope you will remember this: *Hope is born when we are willing to die for the right things.*

This book is the story of an unexpected cardiac crisis in my life that became the unanticipated paradigm for the transformation that God would perform in a century-old, mainline, urban-center congregation. I call it "congregational cardiology" because the process of transformation at Hyde Park United Methodist Church has gone all the way to the heart of our life together. In that process, the central lesson we've been learning is that the only way that leads to life is the way that leads through death. When Jesus said, "Unless a grain of wheat falls into the earth and dies, it remains just a single grain; but if it dies, it bears much fruit" (John 12:24), he was not only defining the central reality of Christian discipleship for individuals, but was also describing a basic principle of life for the church. We will never be ready to live until we confront the possibility of death. Saint Francis of Assisi taught us that "it is in dying that we are born to eternal life." The way of costly obedience is the way that leads to joy.

Why we so often avoid, ignore, or attempt to soften this fundamental theme of the gospel is beyond me. My guess is that it's because the process scares the living daylights out of us! But the followers of a crucified and Risen Lord should be the first people to understand that the only way to find new life is to follow a path that leads through some kind of death. L. Gregory Jones, Dean of the Duke Divinity School, described this process of death and resurrection as the essential characteristic of the Christian life. "As we participate in Christ's dying *and* rising, we die to our old selves and find a future not bound by the past. The focus of this dying and rising is the Christian practice of baptism and it also involves a lifelong practice of living into that baptism, of daily dying to old selves and living into the promise of an embodied new life" (*Embodying Forgiveness*, p. 4, italics his).

The sad reality is that many congregations are so afraid of dying that dying is about the only thing they can do. Worse yet, many are terminally infected with petty, small-time ailments when they could be raised to new life if they were willing to face the risk of death for things that really matter: what they believe, who they are, and the mission God is calling them to fulfill. Robert A. Chestnut, who led the transformation of East Liberty Presbyterian Church in Pittsburgh, says these congregations are controlled by what he calls "long-time, locked-in leadership elites that really would rather see their churches die than change" (*Transforming the Mainline Church*, p. 22).

I recently heard the story of a century-old, downtown church that had been in steady decline for more than two decades. A few visionary leaders saw new possibilities for that building to become the site for creative outreach ministries designed to relate to the new population that was moving back into the urban core. The fulfillment of that vision, however, involved a merger with a rapidly growing congregation several blocks away. In effect, the declining congregation would be absorbed into the growing one so that the downtown property could become a site for expanded ministry to the community. The vision never became a reality because the people in the declining congregation were more willing to die with their past identity intact than to live into the future with a new one. The irony is that if they had been willing to die, they would have found new life. By refusing to die to their past in the present, they ensured their decline and death in the future.

By contrast, Chestnut uses the New Testament word *metanoia,* meaning repentance or conversion, to describe what it meant for East Liberty Presbyterian Church to move in a new direction. "The life of faith begins with a spiritual death to one's old self, old ways, old attitudes, old values. In faith, one is raised up with Christ to new life, new ways and values and attitudes and priorities" (*Transforming the Mainline Church*, p. 13). It will take several chapters to tell the story of how that happened—and continues to happen!—in the heart of our congregation, but we are learning that the Christian life is all about dying and rising again, which is, after all, exactly what Jesus did! And it's a process that goes all the way to the heart.

The statistical evidence of heart disease in America today confirms that most of us avoid dealing with matters of the heart until they become matters of survival. It's

> *How do you understand Jesus' words about the seed going into the ground? What does that image mean for you and for your congregation?*

not as if we don't know better. The American Heart Association could not declare the warnings more clearly. We know the dangers of heart disease. We know the factors that contribute to it. We know what we should do to avoid it: quit smoking, scratch the junk food from our diet, get into the gym for some aerobic exercise, find healthier ways to deal with stress. But when push comes to shove, most of us need to be shoved! Millions of Americans don't make the lifestyle changes that would result in a healthier heart until they find themselves in a cardiac intensive care unit facing major surgery. We do cosmetic patch and repair jobs that improve things for a little while or make things look better on the outside, but we tend to avoid the deeper matter of a change of heart.

If only we were more like the biblical writers! They never dodged the matters of the heart. The word "heart" appears 592 times in Scripture. You could say that the Bible is one long, divinely inspired electrocardiogram. In Scripture, the heart represents the life-giving core of human life. It's like the "mission control center" in Houston that guides the space shuttle in its orbit. The heart is the motivating, controlling center of our human personality, the deep inner source of passion, energy, and direction for our lives. The writer of the Old Testament book of Proverbs captures the overall importance of this theme when he challenges us to "keep your heart with all vigilance, for from it flow the springs of life" (Proverbs 4:23). With unwavering clarity, the Scriptures take us to the deepest places of the heart, convinced that the heart of the matter is always a matter of the heart.

The prophet Ezekiel received a physiological vision of the transformation God intends for human life when he heard the Spirit say, "A new heart I will give you, and a new spirit I will put within you; and I will remove from your body the heart of stone and give you a heart of flesh. I will put my spirit within you, and . . . you shall live in the land that I gave to your ancestors; and you shall be my people, and I will be your God" (Ezekiel 36:26-28).

The surprise that God had in store for us was that the prophetic prescription of divine cardiology applies not only to human beings, but to congregations as well. We were almost involuntarily drawn into a process of congregational cardiology by which God transformed the heart of our life together so that we could live in the land that our ancestors gave us and become the people God was calling us to be.

I share the story of the way God has been at work in the life of Hyde Park United Methodist Church with no illusion that the process of congregation cardiology has been completed in us, that we have learned all of the lessons we need to learn, or that we have found a process of heart transformation that will work for everyone else. I offer it in the spirit of the New Testament witness who wrote, "What we have heard, what we have seen with our eyes, what we have looked at and touched with our hands, concerning the word of life . . . we declare to you . . . so that our joy may be complete" (1 John 1:1-4). If the story of what we have seen, touched, and handled of the word of life is a source of encouragement for you and for your congregation, then our joy will be complete. I also hope that the telling of this story will be an invitation for other congregations to enter into the often risky, always costly, usually painful, but ultimately joyful way through death that Jesus said is the only way to find new life.

So that you have some idea of what you got yourself into by picking up this book, let me share three motivating convictions for ministry that have grown out of our experience.

> *What is your working under-standing of the biblical image of the "heart"? How does that biblical language speak to your experience with God?*

1. The Hope for the Transformation of the World Is in the Local Church

I write from the perspective of more than three decades of ministry as a pastor in The United Methodist Church. I value the corporate strength and common identity of the mainline, denominational churches. Having served at every level of my own denominational structure, I know that Charles Ferguson got it right when he subtitled his history of American Methodism "Organizing to Beat the Devil" (*Methodists and the Making of America*, Eakin Press, 1983). If well-organized programs, agonizingly debated resolutions, carefully crafted strategic plans, nobly inspired good intentions, and truckloads of denominational dollars could bring about the revitalization of the church and transformation to the world, we American Methodists would have accomplished it long ago! It's becoming painfully obvious to just about everyone in them that with a few, notable exceptions, those hulking institutional structures simply aren't working anymore. An old, country proverb says, "If the horse you are riding dies, dismount." The seismic shifts in our culture make institutionally driven, top-down transformation less likely and far more costly than ever before.

I share Bill Easum and Tom Bandy's confidence that "there is great hope for individual churches with the courage to be reorganized, redirected, and systemically transformed" (*Growing*

Spiritual Redwoods, p. 16). I am convinced that the hope for spiritual and social transformation resides in local congregations where people experience new life in Christ and become a part of the fulfillment of God's mission in the world. Like new sprouts breaking through the forest floor, new life comes from the ground up, not from the top down.

There's nothing new about the way the Spirit brings new life from the ground up. Acts 15 records the minutes of the first church-wide council in the history of the Christian movement. Methodists would call a "conference." Baptists would hold a "convention." For Lutherans it would be a "synod." Whatever you choose to call it, the delegates gathered in response to changes that were already taking place in local congregations throughout Antioch, Syria, and Cilicia (Acts 15:23). Gentiles were hearing the good news of God's love in Christ, being baptized, and becoming a part of the mission of the church without becoming Jews by circumcision prior to their baptism.

The apostles and elders, that is, the hierarchy at "denominational headquarters" in Jerusalem, had all been faithful Jews before their experience with Christ. They thought the newly converted Gentiles also should be circumcised. It was obviously a conviction that excluded women along with Gentiles in a very tangible reversal of the message Peter had declared on Pentecost: "I will pour out my Spirit on all people. Your sons and daughters will prophesy . . . even on my servants, both men and women, I will pour out my Spirit" (Acts 2:17-18 NIV).

Luke's description of the council at Jerusalem sounds a lot like most of the denominational conferences I've attended. Luke records that "after there had been much debate," Peter took the floor to declare that "God, who knows the human heart, testified to them by giving them the Holy Spirit, just as he did to us; and in cleansing their hearts by faith he has made no distinction between them and us." He raised a powerful, rhetorical question: "Why are you putting God to the test by placing on the neck of the disciples a yoke that neither our ancestors nor we have been able to bear?" (Acts 15:7-10). With that question hanging in the air, Barnabas and Paul presented the evidence of "all the signs and wonders that God had done through them among the Gentiles" (Acts 15:12). Finally, based on the evidence of God's Spirit at work in local congregations, the council decided, albeit a little grudgingly, that they should "not make it difficult for the Gentiles who are turning to God" (Acts 15:19 NIV).

It was the first—though certainly not the last!—turning point in the path of church history when the institutional hierarchy had to play catch-up with a movement of the Spirit that had already taken place in local congregations. In fact, almost every major movement for renewal and change in the two thousand years of church history came from outside the authoritative structures of official church bodies. When the evidence of transformation became unavoidably clear, the authorities at the top of the church's institutional structure finally affirmed it and gave official support to what the Holy Spirit had already been doing.

Across the country today, the Holy Spirit is at work in vibrant, local congregations of all shapes and sizes to bring new life to the people and communities they serve. A six-year study of the three national Lutheran denominations came to the conclusion that "solutions are found within individual, motivated congregations taken one at a time" (*Church Membership Initiative*, quoted in *Leading Change in the Congregation*,

> *Do you really believe that the hope for God's transformation of the world is in the local church?*

p. 8). The compelling evidence is that the hope for the fulfillment of the vision of God's kingdom, coming on earth as it is in heaven, resides in congregations where ordinary people receive a new heart and are sent into the world as the extraordinary agents of the reign and rule of God.

2. There Is New Hope for Old Congregations

I rejoice in the witness of cutting edge, entrepreneurial, megachurches in the bustling new suburbs of our urban areas. I had the joy of serving as the founding pastor of one of those congregations. In 1979 St. Luke's United Methodist Church at Windermere was planted in the rapidly growing, high-energy communities nestled between Walt Disney World and Universal Studios in Orlando, Florida. It has become one of the most rapidly growing United Methodist congregations in the Southeastern United States. Some of those cutting edge congregations are teaching the rest of us how to communicate the gospel in the twenty-first century. Every growing congregation I know is learning from the examples set by Willow Creek, Saddleback, Ginghamsburg, Windsor Village, or Frazier Memorial, to name a few.

But then, in 1992, I was appointed to serve an urban-center congregation that had been in ministry on the same corner for ninety-three years. The contrast between the two settings could hardly have been more profound. A decade later, I am more deeply convinced than ever before that all of God's work in this world cannot be accomplished in new, megaministry congregations. Both experience and observation have led me to believe that a significant part of God's transformation of the world may yet come through long-established congregations that discover a new heart for mission and ministry. While I believe that the same principles of "congregational cardiology" are at work in newly established churches, this book tells the story of how new life emerged out of the spiritual roots of a long-established one.

The good news is that there is ample evidence that when pastors and laypersons allow the Spirit of God to do a work of divine cardiology in their life together, it is possible for congregations of all kinds of sizes in all kinds of places to become the agents of all kinds of new life. They are scattered all across the country. Their size, mission emphasis, congregational identity, and theological focus are as varied as the communities they are called to serve and the traditions from which they come. Some would be considered "conservative," while others would be identified as "liberal." Some are loaded with Gen-Xers while others are filled with people with gray hair. Some are in expanding suburbs, some are in urban centers, and some are tucked away in quaint rural villages. Some have great financial resources, while others are struggling to make ends meet. The common denominator in all of them is a transformed heart, a clear sense of mission, and a passion for transformation in the lives of people and in the community they serve.

3. Now Is the Time!

The prophet Isaiah could see God doing a new thing in his world. The critical question was whether or not the covenant people could perceive it (Isaiah 43:19). In the same way, God is clearly doing a new thing in our world today through local congregations that are responsive to the movement of the Spirit and faithful to the vision of the kingdom of God revealed in Jesus Christ. The critical question is whether we will see it and allow ourselves to become a part of it. When Dick Wills tells the story of the transformation at Christ Church United Methodist in Fort Lauderdale, he says that one of the decisive moments in the process was when he stopped asking God to bless what they were already doing and started asking God to allow them to become a part of what God was already blessing (*Waking to God's Dream*, p. 32). It is the call to get on board with what God is already doing in the world around us. It's all about learning to die in order to be raised to new life. And it's all a matter of the heart.

- How's your heart? What is going on in the heart of your congregation?
- What do you hope to discover in reading this book?

CHAPTER 2

You Only Have to Die

He was indeed so ill that he nearly died. But God had mercy on him.
—Philippians 2:27

The key to becoming a Spirit-energized, people-loving, life-giving, community-transforming congregation is really very simple. All you have to do is be willing to die.

Looking back, I guess I should have seen the warning signs along the way. There was the morning I was jogging down Bayshore Boulevard, which runs along the Hillsborough Bay in Tampa. About half a mile from home, I had to stop and sit down on a bus stop bench to catch my breath. When I saw my wife drive past on her way to work, I wished I had been able to wave her down to give me a ride. I blamed it on my asthmatic condition, but it was enough to give me some concern. There were other times when I felt a strange blip in my heartbeat but assumed it was a result of too many cups of coffee dumping too much caffeine into my system.

When the irregular heartbeats became more intense, I placed a call to the office of a cardiologist who is a member of our church. When I asked the receptionist for an appointment, she told me in no uncertain terms that the doctor only took patients by referral. Another week or two went by. When the irregular heartbeats could no longer be ignored, I called his office again. This time, with an appropriate measure of pastoral urgency in my voice, I told the receptionist that I was the doctor's pastor and needed to speak with him. In no time, he was on the line. When I told him what I was feeling, he told me to come right in and he'd check me out. It's all who you know in this world!

Twenty-four hours on a heart monitor confirmed that I was in atrial fibrillation. He gave me some medication and told me to call him if there was any change. A day later, I knew the condition was getting worse. The irregular beats had not stopped. I was having a hard time getting my breath. I felt weak and tired. When I went back into the office, he took one look at my blood pressure, listened to my heart, and told me that I was in congestive heart failure and that he wanted to put me in the hospital. I said I could probably do that on Monday. It was Friday afternoon, after all. Sunday was our stewardship commitment service and I really needed to preach that day. In addition, it was Parents' Weekend for my daughter's sorority at the University of Florida and we were planning to be there all day Saturday. He listened politely and then said, "No. I mean right now. I'll see you there as soon as they get you checked in."

The initial diagnosis was cardiomyopathy, a virus-like condition that causes the heart muscle to become incapable of contracting, like a rubber band that loses its elasticity. It can cause the heart to become what Ezekiel, the Old Testament prophet, described as a "heart of stone" (Ezekiel 36:26). The cardiologist told me that the only medical cure was a heart transplant, but before we got to that point we would do a cardiac catheterization to find out exactly what was going on in there and see what we could do.

My cardiologist/parishioner said that in contrast to heart attacks, this heart ailment is not brought on by stress. I'm confident that he was medically correct, but there's a part of me that has never quite believed it. I'm more like the Old Testament Hebrews who saw no separation among mind, body, and spirit, than the Greeks who would later view them as seperate entities. I was forty-five years old. I had recently come through a classic midlife crisis and had written a book to recommend it (*Men at Midlife,* 1992). My wife and I had recently become "empty nesters" after sending our second daughter away to college. I had just come through the most significant career change in my life, which involved profound feelings of loss and separation. I was facing a challenging situation in the church to which I had been appointed. My wife had given up an excellent teaching position for one that was much less satisfying. It sounded like stress to me!

November means football season in Florida. We had planned to spend Saturday watching the University of Florida Gators take on the South Carolina Gamecocks at Florida Field. We had accepted an invitation to join some old friends in a corporate box to watch the Tampa Bay Buccaneers after worship on Sunday. Instead of watching football, I was watching the monitor to see if my heart would go back into normal rhythm so that I could avoid the jolt I had seen on *ER* when Dr. Green put the paddles on a patient's chest and shouted, "Clear!" When my twin brother called from Tennessee to see how I was doing, I said, "I feel like a football player in the locker room at halftime. I really hope I get to play the rest of the game, but if I don't, it's been one hell of a good first half!" It was a somewhat nonpastoral way of saying that, although I knew I could die, I felt deep peace and profound gratitude for the life I had lived. I wanted this life to go on, but if this was the end of the game, I couldn't complain about my time on the field. By the way, the Gators won that weekend and the Bucs lost. In football terms, I was hitting 50 percent!

The news of my condition went out through the United Methodist connection around the country, and people began to pray for my healing. I remember receiving a call from my good friend and fellow pastor, Dick Wills. He was in a clergy meeting in South Florida where someone had just announced that I was in terminal condition and would be having a heart transplant. I told Dick that although I appreciated the concern and was grateful for the prayers, I felt a little like Mark Twain who, when his name mistakenly appeared in the obituary column, supposedly said that the reports of his death were slightly exaggerated.

In short, I didn't have a transplant and I didn't die. We attacked the problem with massive doses of steroids, combined with equally massive doses of prayer. Six months later, my heart was back to normal. About a year later, during one of my checkups, the cardiac technician said, "Jim, I don't think you realize just how bad you were. Most patients who come in here in the shape you were in are told to go home and get their papers in order." She said that most cardiologists would have looked at the reports and said that there was nothing they could do, but that my doctor had decided to take an aggressive approach and see what would happen. When my cardiologist came in that day, I said, "I've finally figured out that I need to thank you for saving my life." He replied, "You'd better thank all those folks who prayed for you because I'm not sure that what we tried did much good."

A couple of years later I was visiting a cardiac patient on the same floor in the same hospital. When his nurse came in, the patient told her about what had happened to me. When she heard my diagnosis, she blurted out, "Most people die with that!" Then she asked if she could listen to my heart. I opened my shirt. She put her stethoscope to my chest, listened for a moment, looked up, and said, "That's miraculous." And it is. It's all very humbling, exceptionally miraculous stuff. God healed my heart of stone and renewed within me a heart of flesh. Ten years later, this skinny old body is in just about the best shape it's ever been. I walk on the Bayshore three days a week, work out regularly at the YMCA, and check in with my cardiologist once a year for old time's sake.

We had no way of knowing at the time that what happened in my heart would become a human analogy to what would happen in our congregation. The changes in store for us involved more than just tinkering around the edges of our life together. That would have done about as much good as rearranging deck chairs on the *Titanic*. The transformation God would perform in us would go all the way to the heart of our identity. It would, in fact, involve the possibility of death—at least the death of some old assumptions and attitudes so that new things might come to life. It would call for hard work and for applying the best lessons we could learn from others. But ultimately, it would be a miraculous work of the Spirit of God in which all of us have been privileged to play a part.

I remember hearing the comedian Flip Wilson say that although beauty may only be skin deep, ugly goes all the way to the bone. The ailment in many long-established, mainline, stable, or declining congregations is not just skin deep. It won't be resolved by congregational cosmetics. The sickness goes all the way to the bone. Thomas Bandy says that declining churches are addicted to "habitual, self-destructive behavior patterns." He declares that "the church cannot simply be renewed—it must be transformed. No programmatic change will overcome addiction" (*Kicking Habits*, p. 15). The factors that keep congregations from experiencing the vitality that the New Testament envisions for them go all the way to the heart of who they are and of who they believe God is calling them to be. If ordinary, standard-brand congregations are ever to become the life-transforming, world-changing Body of Christ, nothing less than congregational cardiology will do.

It's no great stretch of the imagination for me to use my experience in the cardiac ward to describe some of the practical steps toward becoming a healthy congregation. See if any of these steps would fit your congregation.

Step 1. Listen to Your Heart

My cardiac crisis began with a mild discomfort in the chest. I felt as if my heartbeat was out of rhythm. Though I did not have physical pain, whenever I was quiet or still I could feel that something just wasn't right. In the same way, most transformation begins with a heart-level sense that something just isn't right—that we are out of harmony with ourselves, with others, or with God.

For me, one of the most profound lines Shakespeare ever wrote comes at the end of *King Lear*, when the Duke of Albany says, "The weight of this sad time we must obey,/Speak what we feel, not what we ought to say." We church folks spend a lot of time and energy speaking "what we ought to say." We've been conditioned to communicate with a subtle form of ecclesiastical dishonesty. Our words sound religious, but they often avoid the deepest truth in our hearts. That's odd, when you think about it, because the biblical writers assume that what goes on in our hearts is just about as close as we will ever get to the truth. The psalmist prayed, "You desire truth in the inward being; therefore teach me wisdom in my secret heart" (Psalm 51:6). It is in the deepest part of our hearts that the Spirit of God speaks the word of truth to us and about us.

> *In the quiet of your own soul, do you feel some discomfort in your heart? Take time to listen to that discomfort and find out what it is. How would you compare the life and ministry of your church to the life and ministry of the early church in the book of Acts? How does the difference or similarity make you feel?*

So, listen to your heart. Listen with your heart. Listen to the truth that the Spirit will speak within the heart of your congregation. Hold a realistic picture of your church life up against the picture the life of the church recorded in the New Testament book of Acts, and dare to speak what you feel.

Step 2. Find Out What's Going On

When the technician told me that the cardiologist wanted me to wear a 24-hour heart monitor, I was tempted to say, "Gee, that's really a little more hassle than I intended. It's probably just something I ate. Let's skip it for now." But the monitor confirmed there was a problem, and a cardiac catheterization determined what the problem actually was. If our churches are to find healing and wholeness in the future, their leaders need to get a good fix on their health right now.

Alan Nelson and Gene Appel point out that "Familiarity often creates blind spots. . . . The longer we attend a church, the less aware we become. . . . Gleaning information solely from within your family is a sure way to create huge blind spots" (*How to*

Change Your Church Without Killing It, p. 33). Though some of the questions you need to ask can be answered by folks who are deeply involved in the congregation, one of the best ways to get a quick reading is to ask visitors what they felt, sensed, or experienced the first time they came to the church property. Or ask a few honest friends to visit your church and report their experience to you. Did they experience a healthy sense of joyful faith and vibrant Christian community? Did the congregation communicate that new people were genuinely welcome? Did the visitors pick up the unmistakable feeling of a congregation that shared a common understanding of who they are and where they are going? Or did the visitors pick up the unmistakable scent of decline and eventual death?

> *Take a careful analysis of what's actually going on beneath the surface of your congregational life. What's the glue that holds it together? What motivates people to be there? Where's the sickness in your congregational system?*

Step 3. Call in the Specialists

Like most folks, I put off calling the doctor. I figured I could get over this myself, which is a lot like attorneys saying that the person who acts as his or her own lawyer has a fool for a client. When I was gasping for breath, I knew I needed help from someone who had listened to a whole lot more hearts than I and might be able to give me some help. When Jeremiah said, "My joy is gone . . . my heart is sick," he called for the doctor. "Is there no balm in Gilead? Is there no physician there?" (Jeremiah 8:18, 22).

When we began to acknowledge that the joy was largely gone from our congregational life and that there was something sick in our heart, we called in the specialists—people who had more experience in congregational transformation than I had. We knew that we needed the guidance of people who could see what it would take for the church to effectively fulfill its mission in the

> *To whom can you turn? Who can help you read the signs and define the ailments in your congregation? Have you done your homework on the current and future trends for vital congregations? Are you willing to learn whatever you can from anyone who might be able to help you, even folks with whom you may have significant theological differences?*

days ahead. We called on people who had led other congregations like ours in the direction that we knew we needed to go. We read books and attended workshops with creative thinkers like Leonard Sweet, Lyle Schaller, Ezra Earl Jones, Rick Warren, Bill Hybels, Bill Easum, and Tom Bandy. In short, we reached out for all the help we could get.

Step 4. Use Your Oxygen

The first thing the nurse did in the hospital was to show me how to use the oxygen line. They said not to wait. If I started to have difficulty breathing, I should start using it right away. It wouldn't cure my heart trouble, but it would keep me breathing until the problem was found.

Congregational life cannot be put on hold until we get our hearts right. We need to have the internal resources to keep things going while we are in the process of transformation. The Greek word for Spirit is *pneuma,* meaning wind or breath. From the first moment of life in Genesis, when God breathed into human beings the breath of life, through the witness of the early church in the New Testament, right down to this present hour, the "oxygen" of the Spirit of God maintains our life along the road to transformation. The English poet Gerard Manley Hopkins wrote:

> There lives the dearest freshness deep down things . . .
> Because the Holy Ghost over the bent
> World broods with warm breast and with ah! bright wings.
> ("God's Grandeur")

28

As you enter the transformation process, it is important to remember that the Holy Spirit of God broods over this bent world and can bring a deep freshness to everything. It's the only way I know to stay alive!

> *Are you open to whatever the Spirit of God might do within you and through you as a part of the renewal or transformation of your congregation?*

Step 5. Take Your Steroids

Unfortunately, the steroids the doctor prescribed for me were not the same steroids used by athletes to pump up their muscles. I'm just as skinny as ever! But the doctor hoped that injecting them into my system would provide the internal power that would overcome the weakness in my heart. I'm sure that it contributed to my healing, but as the cardiologist confirmed, the strength that actually healed my heart was the divine power that is released through prayer. I know that I am alive today because people prayed for me. And I am just as sure that the new life that has come to our congregation is ultimately not because of what I have done as a pastoral leader, or what other staff or laypersons have done in the congregation. Ultimately, the only hope for new life in any congregation is a massive infusion of the power and presence of the Spirit of God, appropriated through consistent, patient listening in prayer.

> *How is your prayer life? How is the prayer life of your congregation? Are you practicing the spiritual disciplines that will create a space in which the power of the Spirit of God might energize your congregation?*

Step 6. Change Your Lifestyle

Although my heart condition was not the result of lifestyle issues, most heart problems are. We smoke. We eat too much fatty food. We get too little exercise. We allow stress to destroy our bodies from the inside out. Every person I know who has recovered from heart disease has made significant changes in lifestyle. I have not become a world class athlete or vegetarian, but I can assure you that my experience has led to healthy changes in my life. I watch what I eat. I exercise regularly. I'm learning the importance of the "Sabbath" and the reason God took a day off after the work of creation. The transformation in my heart has resulted in practical changes in my lifestyle. And that certainly has been true for us as a congregation. The change in our congregational heart has resulted in significant changes in the way we live together, make decisions, choose the things we do and the things we do not do, and the way we relate to one another.

In the liturgy for the Sacrament of Baptism, we say to the congregation, "Remember your baptism and be thankful." We're not asking them to remember a specific event in the past, but to remember that they are marked by the sign of baptism. As part of the Body of Christ, they are a baptized people whose life together is constantly being transformed by the grace of God that invites them into the continual process of death and resurrection. In the words of Charles Wesley, we are always being "changed from glory into glory."

Are you willing to make the changes that will be necessary for your congregation to become a vibrant, healthy, life-giving expression of the Kingdom of God? Are you open to the kind of changes that prayer can bring?

I love the old story of the woman who placed a magnet on the refrigerator that said, "Prayer changes things." Before the day was over, her husband had taken it down. She asked, "What's wrong with you? Don't you like prayer?" The husband replied, "Sure, I like prayer. I just don't like change!"

Here's the truth: I could have died. But God had mercy on me. God's healing power moved into my heart and restored me to health. And here's the truth about Hyde Park Church. We could have died, or, at best, we could have continued to maintain stability, which would have resulted in decline and eventual death. But God had mercy on us. God's Spirit moved into the deepest part of our life together and gave us a new heart.

In the then-revolutionary 1970s Broadway classic, *Jesus Christ Superstar*, Jesus tells his disciples "You only have to die." That's still all it takes!

CHAPTER 3

For the Sake of the Call

My fate cries out . . . Still am I call'd?
—Hamlet, Act 1, Scene 4

The telephone call came unexpectedly on my forty-fifth birth-day, though the calendar for that March Monday was far too crowded for any celebration of a midlife mile marker. My wife, Marsha, and I were catching a quick bite of supper before I headed back to the church for a meeting of the Staff-Parish Relations Committee. The district superintendent was on the line, telling me that the bishop wanted us to come to his office later that evening. For a Methodist preacher, a call like that at that time of year can only mean one thing. The bishop wanted us to move to another pastoral appointment.

We had been serving St. Luke's United Methodist Church at Windermere, Florida, for thirteen years. By traditional Methodist standards that would have seemed like a long appointment, but we had every expectation of serving there for several more years. As the church's founding pastor, I had seen that congregation grow into one of the most exciting churches in the state. We were constantly catching fresh visions of new opportunities for min-istry in the years ahead. We had recently completed a major building program and were gearing up for another one. When other pastors asked why I had stayed so long, I told them that it was either because no other church wanted me or no other preacher wanted to tackle our debt!

There was another reason we expected to continue to serve there. The committee meeting that evening would give final approval to the appointment of a new associate pastor who happened to be African American. When he joined the clergywoman who was already serving with us, we would become the most inclusive pastoral team in Florida United Methodism. It was a major step in the fulfillment of our mission and one in which the bishop had been actively involved. Unable to say anything about the phone call I had just received, I sat through the meeting facing the possibility that our visit with the bishop would significantly alter the decision we were making.

On the way to the bishop's office, my wife and I tried to guess where he might be asking us to go. Tampa was not even on our radar screen. The only thing I knew about Tampa was how to find Busch Gardens and how to drive through it to visit my in-laws on the other side of Tampa Bay. I knew Hyde Park was one of the historic churches of Florida Methodism, located in the inner core of one of the oldest cites in the state. Compared to the bustling new suburbs we were serving, that fact alone made it just about as radical a change as anyone could imagine. Although I had never had any contact with the congregation, I knew that it was significantly smaller than the one I was serving. I had heard that the current pastor, who had only been there for two years, had health problems, but I had no way of knowing that he would be taking disability leave that year.

During the meeting with the bishop, I asked rather pointedly why we should go to a church with half the worship attendance, half the staff, and half the budget of the church I was serving. The answer had something to do with the potential for growth and the influence of the church in the city. There were other questions and answers, but as the conversation went on, I began to sense that there was more going on here than a request from the bishop. Through the human conversations around the conference table, I began to sense something that could only be defined as the Spirit of God nudging me to say yes.

It was almost 11:00 P.M. when we left to go home. I asked how much time we had to think and pray about the decision. The bishop said he needed to hear from us first thing in the morning.

One of the most important decisions of our lives would be made with no time to gather information, no time to check things out with clergy friends, no time for a clandestine reconnaissance tour of the neighborhood and parsonage. All we could do was pray about it overnight and call in the morning.

I asked the bishop whether he was askin' or tellin'. He said he was asking and that we were free to say no. The truth is that if we had known more about what was ahead of us, we might have turned the appointment down. And, to tell the whole truth, if some of the folks at Hyde Park had known me as well then as they would get to know me in the days ahead, they might have turned me down, too! All I knew was that something about the bishop's request felt like a call from God. One of the truths that had been ingrained in my early spiritual formation is that when God calls, the only appropriate response is to say yes. Somewhere along the way I had learned that the only path to real joy is the path of obedience.

With very little tangible information, without a clue as to what was ahead, and with lots of good reasons not to do it, we said yes because we wanted to be obedient to what we perceived to be the call of God.

Some of my friends were more aware of what the move might mean than I was. One clergy friend sent me a CD by contemporary Christian musician, Stephen Curtis Chapman. The title song captured the kind of obedience that was at the heart of our decision. The haunting refrain simply would not let me go.

> We will abandon it all for the sake of the call
> No other reason at all but the sake of the call.

Leaving St. Luke's Church would be the most painful change in our lives, in part because of the personal investment we had made in birthing that congregation and, in part, because it was where we had raised our daughters, both of whom were now in college. But from the earliest days of that congregation's life, we had worked intentionally to develop a spiritually and emotionally healthy place; a community in which people could laugh and cry; a place where people could speak what they felt, not what they thought they ought to say. As a result, we did our "grief work" very well. In my closing words to the congregation I quoted Emily Dickinson:

> To make Routine a Stimulus
> Remember it can cease—
> Capacity to Terminate
> Is a Specific Grace—
> (www.americanpoems.com/poets/emilydickinson/1196.shtml)

We discovered that there is a specific work of God's grace in what Paul described when he said he was "forgetting what lies behind and straining forward to what lies ahead" (Philippians 3:13). It's a lesson I learned from O. Dean Martin, one of my pastoral mentors. Until his untimely death with cancer, Dean was the outstanding pastor of Trinity United Methodist Church in Gainesville, Florida, and chaplain to the University of Florida Gator football team. He had a knack for communicating big ideas with small images. He could wrap up the whole theme of a sermon in its title. One of his most memorable titles was "Why Windshields Are Larger Than Rearview Mirrors," a title that I stole for one of my last sermons at St. Luke's. They are, of course. Windshields really are significantly larger than rearview mirrors. That's not to say that mirrors aren't important. We can't get along without them. They're so important that they're required by law. We need to know where we have been. But when you're headed down the road, it's more important to see where you are going than where you've been.

There is solid biblical truth behind that analogy. The angelic command to the women at the tomb on that first resurrection morning was, "Go, tell his disciples and Peter that he is going ahead of you to Galilee; there you will see him" (Mark 16:7). The Risen Christ is always out ahead of his disciples, calling them to join him along the road that leads to the future. We need rearview mirrors; we dare not forget the things that have shaped and nurtured our lives. But as followers of a risen Lord, the most important things are always on the road ahead of us. It's always out there, on the road to the future, that we will find him.

A windshield sense of the future is a central part of my understanding of God's call. The result is that a future-focused sense of God's call to Hyde Park has never gone away. There were days I questioned it, days I wondered why the call had come, days I wasn't at all sure where it was going, but never for a day has that sense of calling gone away. That deep, inner sense of God's call kept me going when the going got rough.

Knowing the difference between windshields and rearview mirrors became a critical part of the transformation process for our congregation. When people are deeply invested in their history, any movement for change must be rooted in a vision of the future that is better than the past. We're all a little like the children of Israel, who sometimes wondered whether they might have been better back in slavery in Egypt and who had to keep being reminded of the freedom of the promised land. In process planning and systems analysis, it's called "a preferred vision of the future." In the life of the faith, it's the vision of the kingdom of God coming on earth as it is already fulfilled in heaven. Dean Martin said it's the difference between windshields and rearview mirrors.

The good news is that obedience to a future-focused sense of God's call always results in joy. Looking back now, seeing what God has done in my life and in the life of Hyde Park Church, and seeing who it has helped me become, I can only give thanks to God that we had the good sense to say yes! Every now and then, when I am walking across the parking lot toward the church buildings, I find myself saying, "Wow! I wouldn't trade what I get to do for any other job in the world!" Not every day has been like that. I had days when I prayed, "Lord, I'm really a nice guy. Why did you get me into this?" But seeing where we are now and what is ahead of us, I feel as grateful as the guy who was playing the tuba the day it rained silver dollars. Even on the hard days, I'm grateful for a deep, abiding sense that I'm right where I am supposed to be, doing what I'm supposed to do. It doesn't get better than that!

I might as well be straight with you. Both my own experience and my observation of other church leaders convince me that congregational cardiology is hard work. The process by which God redefines the mission and reenergizes the heart of a local church is a daunting task. I can't imagine tackling it without an unmistakable sense of God's call. Don't leave home without it!

Before moving any farther down this path, let me encourage you to respond to the following questions.

- Where can you identify with this story?
- When have you experienced a clear sense of a divine call as a follower of Jesus? How pervasive is the clarity of God's calling in the life of your congregation?
- What would it mean for you to die to something in your past so that God's call for your future might be fulfilled? How have you discovered the "capacity to terminate" to be a "specific grace"?
- What practical changes would you make if you were to follow Paul in saying: "Not that I have already obtained this or have already reached the goal; but I press on to make it my own, because Christ Jesus has made me his own. Beloved, I do not consider that I have made it my own; but this one thing I do: forgetting what lies behind and straining forward to what lies ahead, I press on toward the goal for the prize of the heavenly call of God in Christ Jesus" (Philippians 3:12-14).
- What difference does it make for you to know that the Risen Christ is going ahead of you and promises to meet you on the road to the future?
- Do you understand how Dag Hammarskjöld felt when he wrote: "To be free, to be able to stand up and leave everything behind—without looking back to say Yes" (*Markings*, p. 91)?

CHAPTER 4

Diagnosis: Congregational Cardiomyopathy

Hope deferred makes the heart sick,
but a desire fulfilled is a tree of life.
—Proverbs 13:12

Let me tell you about James L. Ferman, Sr. He died while I was completing this book, on his eighty-eighth birthday, with his pastors and family by his side. He handed down to his son and grandchildren one of the oldest family-owned automotive dealerships in the nation. The business started over one hundred years ago in a bicycle shop that became the first automotive dealership in Tampa. The Ferman Motor Car Company is one of the best known names in the Tampa Bay area, widely respected for its integrity and its generosity in the community.

A few years ago I was invited to a luncheon celebrating Jim Ferman's fiftieth year as a Chevrolet dealer. Although the dealerships now offer a wide array of cars, in his heart, he had always seen himself as a Chevrolet dealer. I was seated at a table with the head of their marketing department. He told me about the way Mr. Ferman would continue to walk around the dealership, asking each salesperson, "Have you sold any cars today?" When he asked my friend that question, he replied, "Well, Mr. Ferman, I don't actually sell the cars. I handle the marketing." To which Mr. Ferman replied, "Well, are you doing your part?"

Jim Ferman knew what business he was in. He was selling

> *What is your business? Why are you here? Would the people of your congregation be able to define a commonly held vision of their life together?*

cars. Everything that goes on in the dealership is measured by how effectively it works toward that goal. That's what you call clarity of mission and purpose. That's what it means to know what is in your heart. That's what it means to align actions and resources around mission. And that's what declining or dying churches generally are missing.

Hyde Park Church was typical of many mainline congregations in America today. When I arrived in 1992 as the twenty-ninth senior pastor in its ninety-three-year history, I found a congregation that had a very clear sense of its past, was somewhat foggy about its present, and didn't have a clue about its future. There was no clearly defined sense of mission and very little clarity about who we were or where God was calling us to go. Throughout the congregation, deeply committed people were highly effective in specific areas of ministry, but there was no unifying vision, no overarching purpose, no commonly held reason for the church's existence except that we had always been there and that we were glad to be together.

That's what I call "congregational cardiomyopathy." It's an ecclesiastic version of the medical condition that hardens the heart muscle so that it is no longer able to function. It's the lack of heart-level clarity and warmhearted passion about God's mission and vision for the congregation. It's a vicious virus that gradually results in a hardening of congregational life so that it ceases to function as a vibrant, life-giving, community-transforming expression of the kingdom of God. Regardless of how many great things a church has done in the past or how many good things it is doing in the present, that central lack of mission and vision always leads to a gradual hardening of the heart in the present and inevitable death in the future.

One symptom of this heart ailment at Hyde Park was that the average worship attendance had remained nearly stable for most of the past twenty years. Another symptom was that no one seemed to notice that the buildings were seriously outdated and had drifted into a benign state of disrepair. Active church members had come to accept the mediocre quality in their physical surroundings as normal. The eighty-four-year-old sanctuary was deeply loved by the congregation, but to a person entering it for the first time, it was downright dingy. The ministry offices were an inefficient cluster of rooms that, in spite of the best efforts of our custodians, never seemed to be clean. There was no fax machine, no answering machine, and the three computers that existed could not communicate with each other. The 1922 vintage education building seeped moisture in its ground floor, leaving the unmistakable scent of mildew throughout its three floors. The buildings were almost totally inaccessible to persons with handicapping conditions. No one seemed to notice that the way most people entered the sanctuary wound past air-conditioning units and trash cans. A visitor would have been hard-pressed to know whether they were coming to worship or taking out the garbage.

The condition of the buildings was symptomatic of mediocrity or benign neglect in other areas of the church's ministry. My first surprise was discovering that the pews still held the former Methodist hymnal, four years after a new one had been published. It was impossible to find an accurate membership roll or mailing list. Although the church said it placed a high priority on evangelism, there was no clearly defined

> *Take a good look around your property for the subtle signs of "congregational cardiomyopathy." Can you find evidence of benign neglect? What would a first-time visitor really see, smell, feel, or experience?*

process for leading people toward commitment to Christ and membership in the church and for forming them as Christian disciples. The church was financially sound, but there was no systematic process for inviting people to make a commitment. My wife (who handles all of the financial matters in our family!) had to ask three times before we were given offering envelopes, and we tithe! The most serious of all the symptoms was that there was limited evidence of a commonly held desire to share the love of God in Christ with persons outside our walls. Some visitors said they experienced a "clubby" atmosphere that seemed to mirror the social structure of the community around us. Members were obviously glad to be there. What was not obvious was whether or not they wanted people who did not fit a specific profile to come in.

Let me hasten to say that Hyde Park was, like all the children in Garrison Keillor's stories of Lake Wobegon, far "above average." Its overall life and ministry were amazingly effective in the lives of the people who were there. The sense of community and compassion within the congregation was unmistakable. There were strong, healthy adult Sunday school classes in which people were growing in their faith and experiencing Christian community. The church was known in the community for the excellence of the classical music that was offered by its Chancel Choir. The loyalty of third- and fourth-generation families bore witness to the church's vitality across the years. Various individuals and groups were actively involved in ministries in the community and were passionately committed to the global mission of the church. And, most important of all, there was within the congregation a deep reservoir of spiritual discipline growing out of the church's long history of faithful witness and ministry. It was, in fact, a healthier, stronger, more vibrant congregation than many if not most other mainline churches in our urban centers. It had many great attributes, but it lacked a commonly shared sense of mission and had no compelling vision for its future.

Within my first months at Hyde Park we made what became the single most important decision of our life together. The "to do" list of things that needed to be improved, updated, or changed could have kept church leaders busy for a long time. Given my hyperactive personality, I could have easily decided to take the list and go to work. There were, in fact, laypersons who wanted to do just that. But as I got to know the congregation, I discovered that the things one person wanted to change were the very things that someone else wanted to keep the same. I also realized that all of these were cosmetic changes over which people might be willing to fight, but none of them would go to the heart of our life together. We decided, instead, to start with our mission. Once we had defined God's calling for us as a congregation, we would have a common criterion for making decisions on what to do and how to do it.

There were, of course, some things we began to do immediately, like updating the membership roll and mailing list, networking the office computers, preparing for a stewardship commitment program, and launching DISCIPLE Bible study. But all of these actions were like using oxygen while the doctors studied my heart condition. They were ways of improving our life together while we worked on what would be most critical to our future.

Church leaders remembered several noble attempts at defining the mission and vision of the church. A layperson who had been involved in every one of those attempts said that it always seemed to come out at the same place. A committee would write some kind of mission statement that would be approved by the administrative board. It would then be placed in a plastic binder and tucked away in a file drawer until a new pastor came along asking about it. No one in the congregation could tell you what that mission statement said and none of the results of those study groups, planning retreats, or workshops seemed to make much difference in what the church actually did. The most recent attempt at a "vision" for the future had resulted in a document that talked about things like the pastors wearing robes in worship and the need for additional rest rooms. It was not exactly the kind of vision that would energize a body of people to creative action!

Because of this history, it was critically important for us to communicate two things from the very beginning of the process. First, in defining the work of the mission and vision task force, we said that their task was not to come up with a mission for the church, but to lead the entire congregation in a process by which we would all listen for God's Spirit to speak to us. Their task was to facilitate the process. The results would belong to the congregation. Second, we said that we intended to define a mission that would actually guide us in making decisions about our future. It would not be tucked away in a plastic folder; it would become the core of our life together.

The process in which the task force led the congregation is the subject of another chapter, but the critical decision was that we would begin with mission and allow our mission to shape our life together. It would become the heart of our identity—the mission control center that would guide us into the future.

When we started that process, we had no way of knowing just how exhausting and exhilarating it would be. I had no idea where it would come out. But we committed ourselves to a process that would go all the way to the heart. Perhaps these questions will help you begin to enter into that heart transformation process in your congregation.

- What difference would it make in your community if your congregation ceased to exist? Who would miss it? What would they miss? Why would they miss it?
- When has your congregation given serious consideration to its mission? What difference did that process make in what you are doing today?
- How long has it been since your church leaders have visited other congregations that are living out of a clear sense of their mission? How aware are you/they of the seismic cultural shifts that have occurred in the past ten years? What was the last book you read or workshop you attended that gave you new visions for ministry?
- How is the spiritual health of your congregation? Is there a vital sense of God's presence? Are your church leaders engaged in vital spiritual discipline and prayer?

CHAPTER 5

Cardiology Is Not for the Fainthearted

To lead is to struggle. In a world such as ours, in history as we know it, to choose the path of leadership is to be on a collision course with conflict.
—Leighton Ford, *Transforming Leadership*

Psychologist Scott Peck opened his longtime bestseller, *The Road Less Traveled*, with the simple declaration: "Life is difficult" (p. 15). Novelist and theologian, Frederick Buechner said that good writers are those who are willing to bleed (*Speak What We Feel*, p. ix). Business consultants James C. Collins and Jerry I. Porras discovered that "visionary companies are not exactly comfortable places" (*Built to Last*, p. 186). Congregational visionary Tom Bandy tells transformational church leaders to "plan for stress" (*Kicking Habits*, p. 17).

From very different perspectives, each of them confirms Jesus' warning, "The road is hard that leads to life" (Matthew 7:14). The unavoidable reality we so often attempt to avoid is that birth always involves pain. Transformation is always difficult. Change always brings stress. The way that leads to new life is always hard.

My guess is that many long-established churches fail to experience the vitality that the New Testament envisions for them simply because they are not willing to face the struggle, feel the pain, or pay the price for new life. The Spirit of God has been teaching us that congregational cardiology is not for the faint-hearted. It can, in fact, be a life or death deal.

Most transformational leaders have already learned this lesson the hard way. A couple of years ago I was invited to share the Hyde Park story in a conference for the leaders of large-membership churches. I was low man on the totem pole, the last speaker on the program. The speakers before me had been upbeat in telling positive stories of dramatic spiritual awakening and effective leadership. It was all very exciting stuff. When I told our story, I acknowledged how difficult the heart transformation process became. I told them that it nearly killed me, that there were days when some folks wondered if it might kill the church. I described the way God brought new life to our congregation when we were willing to die for the things that mattered most. I told them that as difficult as it was, seeing who this church is becoming today is more than worth the price we paid.

At the conclusion of the session, I was surrounded by church leaders who were going through the same things. Some, with tears in their eyes, said they were about to give up. For them, the upbeat success stories felt like offering water to a drowning swimmer. They were really glad to know that they were not alone in their struggle, that sometimes the going gets rough, but that it's worth it in the end.

More recently, I was asked to introduce my book, *Journey to the Center of the Faith*, to a regional gathering of pastors. Because the book emerged out of the process I'm describing in this book, I shared the abridged version of our story. Again, when the meeting ended, pastors were standing in line to share the difficult days they were facing. In both settings, we discovered what Paul meant when he wrote, "you are having the same struggle that you saw I had and now hear that I still have" (Philippians 1:30). In sharing our common pain, new hope was born. Listening to the experience of other leaders, I have become convinced that any long-established congregation that gets serious about finding God's mission and vision for its future is headed for what Leighton Ford described as "a collision course with conflict" (*Transforming Leadership*, p. 251).

When I arrived at Hyde Park, I found a warmhearted congregation that had deep appreciation for its past, was foggy about its mission in the present, and lacked a guiding vision for its future. That lack of clarity about who we were and where we were going enabled us to pretend that we all shared a common understanding of the faith and lived out of a common commitment. But as I began to feel the pulse of the congregation by visiting with people and listening to their stories, I found that beneath the surface of polite, Southern piety, we were a very disparate group of people.

Where have you experienced tension or conflict in your ministry? How have you shared that struggle with others who face the same thing?

We held to very different understandings of the faith and operated under very diverse and sometimes conflicting assumptions about the mission of the church.

I soon learned a lesson that no seminary professor ever taught me. As long as a congregation's mission is vague or undefined, people can get along pretty well by pretending that the church is what they believe it to be. But if you begin defining your identity or searching for God's vision for the future, some faithful, deeply committed people will stand up and cheer, while other equally faithful and equally committed people will either rise up in protest or stand up and walk. Clarity of mission forces people to decide whether or not the mission of this particular congregation is something they can affirm and share.

In our case, the lightning rod was theological and denominational identity. No one had told me that in recent years the leadership of the congregation had taken a sharp turn to the theological right. Several of the members who controlled the decision-making bodies in the congregation defined their faith in the terms of classic Christian fundamentalism, following the contemporary expression of the fundamentalist movements of the early twentieth century. They held very conservative views of the inspiration of Scripture, the nature of salvation, and the mission of the church. They acknowledged our congregation's historical roots, but they were not at all sure that they really wanted to be identified with our denomination. I was surprised to discover that one of the reasons the pew racks still held the now out-of-print hymnal was because some leaders wanted to purchase a nondenominational one.

It's important for me to say that these were good people who were deeply committed to Christ, disciplined in their study of Scripture, and very clear about their convictions. It's also important to say that Christians on the theological left can be just as rigid, unbending, and hard-hearted as those on the theological right. While working on this chapter I visited a pastor who is facing a similar struggle with a very rigid group of people on the theological left. I've experienced it at denominational gatherings in which the people on the far left and the far right are equally intransigent and equally devoid of a loving, tender, Christlike heart. Because they take themselves so seriously, fundamentalists are no fun, regardless of where they stand on the liberal-conservative continuum. Hardness of the heart is not the exclusive ailment of any one theological perspective.

I soon discovered that although they wielded a significant amount of power, the self-defined fundamentalists at Hyde Park did not represent the congregation as a whole. Most of our folks were mainline, warmhearted, gracious Christian people in the Southern, evangelical, Methodist tradition. They took their faith and convictions seriously, but they were open to the possibility that other faithful Christian people might see things differently than they did. By contrast, some of the more conservative folks were very sure that they were Christians, but they weren't at all sure about the rest of us. They held a vision of the church as a small, inner circle of "true Christians" who believed exactly what they believed the way they believed it, surrounded by a larger circle of people whose faith they seriously questioned. One person told me that as he watched people go forward to receive communion, he tried to determine which ones were "real" Christians and which were not.

My message to the more conservative people was always the same. "There's room in this church for you," I'd tell them. "All

I'm asking is that you allow a few inches of space for other folks to be equally committed to Christ but to see some things differently than you do." I knew, of course, that I was asking for the one thing that

> *How have you experienced "hardness of heart" in your congregation? In yourself?*

fundamentalists of any persuasion are totally incapable of doing.

There were many points of tension along the way, but a few became defining moments for us. In my first meeting with the Committee on Nominations, one of the most deeply respected, longtime members of the church surprised me by saying that she thought it was about time this church had a woman in the position of Lay Leader. I've always loved her for that and sort of wished that I had been smart enough to set her up to do it! Another woman turned directly to me and asked, "Well, Pastor, what do you think about that? Doesn't the Bible say that women should not be in any position that would place them in leadership over men?" It was not exactly the time or place to go into a detailed discussion of the biblical understanding of women's roles in the church, so I simply said that I did not see a biblical problem with it and thought it was a good suggestion. The rest of the committee supported the idea and nominated a respected woman as Lay Leader. She was elected by the Church Conference that fall without hesitation.

Then there was the time I recommended Leslie Weatherhead's classic, *The Christian Agnostic*, to one of our members who was struggling with his faith. While I don't agree with everything in the book, I knew that Weatherhead's approach would be a good starting point for his spiritual journey. He liked the book so much that he recommended that his Sunday school class discuss it.

The title alone was enough to send some of our more conservative brothers and sisters into apoplexy. The next thing I knew, it showed up on the agenda for the Staff-Parish Relations Committee. After listening to several complaints about a Sunday school class using the book, one member asked why the Personnel Committee of the church was discussing what an adult group was reading. That's when I spoke up. "It's because I recommended it," I said. "Frankly, I don't agree with everything in the book, but I recommended it as prescription medicine for a particular need. The reason it's being brought up here is because some folks are unhappy that the pastor would recommend it. It's all about pastoral leadership."

There was some vigorous discussion about the book, about my role in recommending it, and about the freedom of adult study groups to select their own material. Finally, the oldest member of the committee, an adult Sunday school teacher who represented a multigenerational family in the congregation, asked to speak. He reached into his briefcase and brought out a well-worn copy of *The Christian Agnostic*. He laid it down on the table and said, "When I came back from World War II, I had seen so many people die that I could hardly believe in God. This book helped me begin to believe again. It would do you all good to read it." With that, there was nothing more to say—to the great disappointment of the folks who were determined to divide the church over the issue.

Another defining moment came in the annual evaluation of my appointment. In the United Methodist system, the Staff-Parish Relations Committee sends an annual report to the bishop recording its vote as to whether the pastor should be reappointed or moved to another appointment. Through more than twenty years of pastoral ministry, I had never received anything other than unanimous support from the committees in the churches I had served.

When the committee asked whether I wanted to say anything before they made their decision, I told them that I believed it was time for them to decide what direction God was calling Hyde Park to go. I said, "If God is calling Hyde Park to be a fundamentalist congregation, you need to be the very best fundamentalist congregation you can be. But I'm not the one to lead you in that direction. I'll be the first to ask the bishop to send me somewhere else. If, on the other hand, you believe that God is calling Hyde Park to be a spiritually alive, warmhearted, Christ-centered congregation that lives out of the center of the Methodist tradition, I'll give you my life to do that. But you have to choose."

It was the first time I had ever placed that kind of ultimatum before a committee, but I'm no dummy. I had been doing my homework. I thought I knew what was in the heart of the congregation. When the votes were counted, there were seven in favor of my reappointment and two in favor of a pastoral change, which I think was a pretty accurate representation of the congregation as a whole.

These decisive moments bear witness to the kind of struggle that was going on in the heart of the congregation. Discussion and dialogue about our mission brought to the table all sorts of concerns that had been tucked away beneath the pews. The truth is that it was painful. It was painful for me because I became the target of some people's unhappiness or frustration. It was painful for people who suddenly discovered that lifelong friends were on the opposite side of the debate. It was painful for the congregation to see people who had been its leaders start to leave, most of them going to a rapidly growing conservative church in our city. It split families when one spouse stayed at Hyde Park and the other went somewhere else. And it was painfully confusing for a large number of folks who simply could not understand what the fuss was about.

The process was also very expensive. Hyde Park had, for a number of years, depended on a few very generous givers to carry most of the financial support of the church. Fundamentalists may not be fun, but they do tithe! In one year, more than $60,000 in pledges walked out the door, forcing us to readjust the budget downward. When these folks began to leave, it caused others to question themselves, which, in the end, was a very good thing. It certainly caused me to question myself and my leadership. There was no escape. We were forced to be very clear about what we believed and to talk very honestly about the direction in which we believed God was calling the church to go. It took us all the way to the heart of our life together.

Lovett Weems says that the task of leaders is not to resolve conflict through victory for one side or compromise for

When have you been forced to go "all the way to the heart" of your life together? What did you find?

the other, but to watch "for God's new creation to emerge. Often a third alternative becomes the 'new thing' God is doing in our midst" (*Leadership in the Wesleyan Spirit*, p. 92). As a leader, I was not able to accomplish that goal, but God did!

When we came through those difficult days, we knew that we had "gone to the mat" for the right reasons. We had struggled with issues that went all the way to the heart of our life together. Having paid the price over those issues, everything else has moved in an absolutely amazing way. Because we paid the price of conflict there, we have had almost no conflict over any of the decisions we have made since. Two years prior to my coming, the congregation was split in a divisive conflict over whether to purchase a new parsonage or renovate the existing one. It was clearly a decision that had more to do with maintenance than mission, but because the mission was foggy, it became a point of great tension. By contrast, in the past seven years we have built new buildings and renovated or torn down old ones on every square inch of our property with nearly unanimous decisions on every project. What's the difference? It's the difference that comes when people have been willing to die for the right things. It's the new sense of common direction that comes when people go all the way to the heart.

The best way I know to invite you to find yourself in our story is to share, as honestly as I can, some of the places where I blew it and some of the places where, by God's grace, I got it right. Perhaps my experience can offer some benchmarks for your leadership.

First, some places where I really blew it.

1. I tended to take things too personally.

Too often, I allowed myself, my faith, and my leadership to be the target of criticism and complaint. G. K. Chesterton supposedly said that angels can fly because they take themselves so lightly. I can see times when things would have gone more smoothly if I had taken myself more lightly. Some of the attacks were very personal, but I wish I had been more consistent in saying, "This really isn't about me. It's about who God is calling this church to be."

Cyrus Vance was a longtime Washington insider who served as Jimmy Carter's Secretary of State. He had a reputation of being a problem solver with a gift for making progress in international stalemates. When he died, *Time* magazine quoted Strobe Talbott, who said, "He is allergic to the first person singular. . . . Because he has so little interest in getting credit, the contending parties are more likely to trust him" (*Time,* March 9, 1992). One of the great dangers for leaders in the transformation process is that we forget that this is really not about us. It's not about credit or blame. It's about God's kingdom coming on earth as it is already fulfilled in heaven, through the life of this local congregation.

2. I let the critics get to me, a.k.a. "losing your cool."

There were times when taking myself too seriously played directly into the hands of the critics and caused me to become part of the conflict. There was the time I cussed, said "damn it" to a chuch member. It was not in public, and I did ask for forgiveness, but I'm sure the word got around. There were times when I was overly defensive, although I learned that just because you're paranoid doesn't mean people aren't out to get you! There were times when instead of attempting to listen more intently, I argued more intensely. And there were times when I was like the preacher who wrote into the margin of his sermon, "Point very weak here. Yell like hell!"

I once heard E. Stanley Jones, one of the most widely respected global Christians of the twentieth century, say that we should allow our harshest critics to become our best teachers. I could have avoided some of the conflict if I had been able to practice that principle more consistently. A United Methodist bishop once told me that he is often tempted to give a one-sentence response to the letters of criticism that come his way: "You could be right."

3. I didn't always go to the source.

Part of the dysfunction in our congregational system was that we did not deal with conflict directly. My most vocal critics never came directly to me. I would get wind of the criticism secondhand or when an unexpected letter of complaint turned up in a committee meeting. One person would tell me something that they had received "in confidence" from someone else, which meant that they would not divulge the name of the person offering the criticism. Simply to break through the camouflage and model a healthier way of dealing with conflict, I wish I had been more direct in calling those persons and saying, "I heard on the grapevine that you are unhappy with me. Let's get together to talk about it." My guess is that some of the conflict would have disappeared if we had faced it directly.

4. I shared too much of myself with the staff before I had a staff I could trust.

I am a pretty open guy who has always had a circle of people with whom I could share my own questions, doubts, and struggles. I thought the church staff was the kind of community in which I could bare my soul and get honest feedback about what was going on in the congregation. Unfortunately, I later discovered that we had not yet reached that level of trust, confidence, or community. Some members of the church staff would go directly to the most vocal critics under the guise of asking that person to pray with them for guidance. Instead of providing honest feedback to avoid conflict, they were allowing my questions to become another piece of ammunition for those who opposed the direction we were going.

Then, there were some places where, by God's grace, I got it right.

1. I felt the pain.

There's danger in telling this story. The danger is that people who are in conflict with one another in a congregation will be too quick to say, "Good riddance!" The danger is that we will let people go or drive them away simply to make life easier for ourselves. To an almost unhealthy degree, I wrestled with each situation in my own heart, searching for anything I might have done differently to heal the rift and keep the congregation together. Ultimately, the separation had to come, and the congregation is healthier and stronger because of it. However, I attempted (very imperfectly!) to stay on the side of reconciliation without compromising my integrity. It's the only way I know to avoid developing a hard heart.

During the most difficult days of the struggle with apartheid in South Africa, Central Methodist Church in Johannesburg became a daring model of the wholeness, justice, and peace of the kingdom of God. But that witness did not come without great pain. When Peter Storey, the pastor who led in the transformation of that congregation, tells the story, he remembers the pain he felt with every white member who left because Central was becoming a mixed race congregation. "I remember how each departure was like a blow in the solar plexus. I felt each one go" (*With God in the Crucible*, p. 95). Like Jeremiah, he felt the pain of the separation without compromising the Kingdom vision that was being born. That's the kind of tenderhearted leadership that models something of the love of Christ in the middle of conflict.

2. I gave up trying to play the critics' game.

I learned the hard way that many of my opponents were better at this game than I was. Some, in fact, had been raised in dysfunctional family systems in which manipulation of conflict was as normal to them as riding a bicycle. Some people had honed their talents to the point that they could stick the knife in, pull it back out, and leave the room without getting a drop of blood on their hands. When I tried to play by their terms or out maneuver them, I always lost. Finally, I simply gave up and decided to be who I am and not try to counter every one of their actions. Thomas Friedman's insights on family systems in his book, *Generation to Generation*, were helpful at this point.

3. I turned to my friends.

I have been a part of a clergy retreat group for nearly twenty years. Their continued support was a great resource for encouragement. But those friends are scattered around the state, and I needed a network that was closer at hand. By God's grace, I was invited to join a group with three other pastors who met once a month for half a day to share our stories and pray for each other. I'll always be grateful for the honest feedback, prayerful wisdom, and joyful strength I received from Tom, Burt, and Jack during those days. I also remained connected to several wise laypersons outside the congregation. I still keep a letter from one of those friends that said, "Just let Jim be Jim and that will be enough." I also developed some trusting relationships with church members who I knew would give me honest feedback. They helped me keep my equilibrium through their understanding of the congregation and their commitment to the vision that was emerging. At the same time, they never let me off the hook. They helped hold me accountable for my own behavior.

4. I asked for forgiveness.

Archbishop Desmond Tutu shared the amazing story of South Africa's Truth and Reconciliation Commission in his book, *No Future Without Forgiveness*. The story demonstrates a way of dealing with conflict that moves beyond the win/lose ideology of the Western world. It's inevitable that when we are involved in conflict, we will need to be forgiven and to ask for forgiveness. Whenever possible, I tried to acknowledge where I had blown it and ask for forgiveness. Basically, I'm a pretty forgiving person.

I can forgive a lot in other people because there are so many times that I need to be forgiven! I offered forgiveness to others and expected them to be able to forgive me. Whether they were capable of returning that forgiveness was up to them. I think that's what the New Testament means by grace.

5. I listened to the sages.

A long-established congregation is blessed by the presence of mature saints who have walked the road of faith, who have been through the struggles, and who see reality through the lens of a deep, abiding faith in God. I turned to these people often, listening to their wisdom, trusting their guidance, and knowing that they would tell me the truth. They became something of a tuning fork for my leadership. I knew that when I was in tune with them, I was in harmony with the Spirit's work in the congregation. I knew that they loved me and loved their church enough to search with me for God's best will for all of us.

6. I paid attention to our history.

This will be the theme of an entire chapter. It's enough to say here that it was important for me to know who the congregation had been across its history and to build the future out of the past. It also meant claiming our denominational identity. I knew I was on the right track when some of the oldest members of the church said, "It feels like we're a Methodist church again." Without being blind to the problems within our denomination, we laid claim to the deepest roots of our spiritual and theological tradition. The hymnal choice, for instance, became very simple. We would either purchase the new United Methodist hymnal, or we would use the old ones until the backs fell off. The solution was to invite anyone who wanted to purchase new hymnals to make a donation for them. In no time, the hymnals had been replaced.

7. I tried to keep laughing.

The second psalm contains one of my favorite descriptions of God: "He who sits in the heavens laughs" (Psalm 2:4). Our congregation had been through years of deep pain. That pain, combined with the natural tendency of fundamentalists to take everything very seriously, resulted in a major deficit of laughter. Whenever possible, I tried to inject a sense of joy and laughter into what felt like the deadly seriousness of our life together. Some folks just couldn't get it, but I treasure the day one of our church leaders, a person of profound faith with a genuine Christlike spirit, brought me a version of the "Serenity Prayer" that read, "Grant me the serenity to accept the things I cannot change, the courage to change the things I can change, and the wisdom to hide the bodies of all the people I had to kill because they really pissed me off." It was just offensive enough to keep me laughing for a long time!

8. We learned to pray.

Times of stress are great opportunities to move into a deeper place of trust, faith, and obedience to God. As the tension increased, I had enough good sense to increase the consistency and depth of personal spiritual discipline. In a later chapter I will describe some of the ways in which we are learning to live and lead out of our life of prayer.

9. I held on.

God has a way of using our human weaknesses to fulfill the divine purpose. That's what Paul was describing when he wrote, "But [the Lord] said to me, 'My grace is sufficient for you, for my power is made perfect in weakness.' So, I will boast all the more gladly of my weaknesses, so that the power of Christ may dwell in me" (2 Corinthians 12:9).

One of my human weaknesses is that I can be very tenacious.

I grew up in a family of world-class debaters. Early on, I learned to hold my ground and wear the opposition down. Across the years, the process of sanctification and the healing of my heart have involved a softening of the abrasive edges of that tenacity. But looking back, I can see ways in which God used that tenacious energy in an amazing way. Low and behold, what this congregation needed at this point in its history was a pastor who would not be too easily swayed by those in power or too easily pushed off course when things got rough. It needed a leader who would not be afraid to ask the hard questions and would not give up until they were answered. There was, however, a critical difference between the times when I held on for the sake of the mission of the church and the times when I held on out of my own insecurity or a personal need to win the debate. Although I long ago received forgiveness for the times when I went overboard in this, I now can see the way God used my natural tenacity to break through the inertia of the past and search for God's direction for our future.

Congregational cardiology is not for fainthearted pastors or lay leaders who are only interested in maintenance ministry. There are maintenance pastors and maintenance congregations, and they need to live together. But looking back across the struggle we went through and seeing how God was at work within it, I find myself singing the African American song that says, "I wouldn't take nothin' for my journey now!"

If God is calling you and your congregation into a process of transformation, I think I can promise you four things.

1. There will be conflict.
2. You will make mistakes.
3. God's grace will be sufficient for you, and God's strength can be at work through your weakness.
4. When the transformation happens, it will be more than worth the price you paid!

CHAPTER 6
Vision Matters

*Vision is not an idealized version of congregational life that [pastors]
must somehow communicate to [their] flock. Vision is the capacity to
see—to comprehend what is going on and to discern how it connects
and relates to the larger narrative of the Christian tradition.*
—David J. Wood, *The Christian Century*

Do you remember that decisive moment in *Alice in
Wonderland* when Alice comes to a fork in the road and doesn't
know which way to turn? She asks the Cheshire Cat which road
to take. He asks where she wants to go. She says she has no idea.
He says that if you don't know where you are going, it really
doesn't matter which road you take. The biblical version of that
principle comes from the Old Testament book of Proverbs, which
declares that "where there is no vision, the people perish"
(Proverbs 29:18 KJV).

The proverb is not true because it's in the Bible; it's in the
Bible because it's true. It's true in business. James Collins and
Jerry Porras confirmed that the corporations that continue to be
effective over time are those who hold to a "core ideology . . .
a set of basic precepts that plant a fixed stake in the ground: 'This
is who we are; this is what we stand for; this is what we're all
about' " (*Built to Last*, p. 54).

It's true in our personal life. United Methodist bishops still ask
every person coming for ordination the same question John
Wesley asked the first Methodist preachers: Are you going on to
perfection? I remember hearing a bishop tell a group of

candidates that if they had trouble saying yes to that question, he wanted to know where they did think they were going.

It's true in the church. When the early Methodists were asked why God had called their movement into being, their answer was, "To reform the nation, particularly the Church, and to spread Scriptural holiness over the land" (www.umc.org/faithinaction /unity/one_voice.htm). And that's exactly what they did!

It was true on the day of Pentecost, when Peter recalled the words of the Old Testament prophet, Joel: "In the last days it will be, God declares, that I will pour out my Spirit upon all flesh, and your sons and your daughters shall prophesy, and your young men shall see visions, and your old men shall dream dreams" (Acts 2:17).

The gift of the Holy Spirit to the early church was the gift of a dream, a Spirit-impregnated vision of God's mission to carry the good news of the love of God in Christ to the whole world. And the continuing work of the Holy Spirit in the church today is to plant that same sense of mission and vision in the heart of every congregation.

It didn't take an exceptional amount of spiritual insight or pastoral brilliance to see that Hyde Park Church needed to catch a fresh vision of its mission for the future. Before we could answer the practical questions about what to do and how to do it, we needed to answer some fundamental questions that went to the heart of our life together.

> Who are we?
> Why are we here?
> What do we believe?
> Who are the people in our community who are not currently committed to Jesus Christ, and what would it take for us to reach them?
> What is God calling us to be and do in this community in our second century of ministry?

I was quite sure that I didn't have the answers to all of those questions. Even more important, I was very sure that the congregation needed to have ownership of the answers. In giving birth to a new congregation, I had discovered that the process of answering those questions was as important as the answers themselves. I also knew that if the process was going to have any authority or credibility, it had to emerge through the existing structures of the congregation. It could not be something I imposed from without; it had to be the congregation's thing, emerging from our life together, growing out of the long history and spiritual tradition of the congregation. More specifically, I knew that decisions for change would need to come through the familiar decision-making process of a congregation that lived by the then Byzantine organizational structures of our United Methodist *Book of Discipline.*

Because our *Discipline* has thankfully been changed to encourage the kind of "mission-based ministry" that we followed and because we hope people in other denominational structures will read this book, there is no particular value in walking through the details of that process. The point is that well-intended, Spirit-energized movements for change often go amuck because an enthusiastic leader tries to do an end run around the existing life and structures of the congregation. In long-established churches, people are more likely to accept change if it comes through familiar decision-making processes.

Our first step was for our annual Church Conference to approve the formation of a "21st Century Task Force." We called it a "task force" rather than a "committee" because the term seemed less threatening to people who might be afraid of change. The purpose of the task force was to lead the congregation in a process of study, dialogue, and prayer by which we could define God's mission and vision for our second century of ministry.

Having received official authorization for the process, I worked carefully with the Committee on Nominations to make sure that this task force included long-term church leaders and newer members, trusted congregational sages and fresh thinkers, and, very specifically, people who were gifted in the planning process and strategic thinking. One of God's answers to our prayers was a new member of the church who had come to lead the Tampa Downtown Partnership and was uniquely gifted in leading group process. Because of his role in the community, he was respected by many of the church's leaders. Because he was new to the congregation, he did not bring a truckload of assumptions to the process. And because of his focus on the process, he was able to draw diverse people into conversation along the way.

Leaders who are ready to begin defining the mission and vision of a congregation today are surrounded by a wealth of resources to assist them in the process, some of which are included in the bibliography. Rather than follow any one model, we shaped our own process by drawing together elements from many sources that seemed most appropriate for our congregation. Here are the steps that contributed to our being in touch with the deepest realities of our community, our church, and our mission. Perhaps they can become "Vision Steps" for you and your congregation.

Vision Step 1: Study

The truth is that many faithful church leaders are largely unaware of a biblical vision of the church. The task force began by studying the book of Acts and the Epistle to the Ephesians in order to root our process in the New Testament images of the church. We then turned to a discussion of the statements on doctrine and mission in the United Methodist *Book of Discipline* to frame our thinking in our spiritual and ecclesial tradition. From there, we turned our attention to current studies of local church life and

> *Vision Questions:*
> *Have you done your homework?*
> *Is your congregation growing in its understanding of the New Testament vision for the Body of Christ?*
> *How well do your leaders understand the spiritual tradition of your denomination?*
> *Are you/they keeping up with the latest resources on congregational life?*

ministry, written by visionary leaders including Lyle Schaller, Leonard I. Sweet, Bill Easum, and Tom Bandy. Our general pattern was for a task force member to read one of the books and then share what he or she had learned and how it might apply to us. Each member of the task force received copies of the notes of those discussions for future reference.

Vision Step 2: Research

While working on this book, I visited with the pastor of a church in a Northern city. In the 1950s and 1960s, it was one of the largest and most influential congregations in its city. In recent years, however, it has been in steady decline. A fundamental shift in the racial and economic demographics of their neighborhood has become the most important single factor in defining their vision for the future. Without that demographic reality check, they might have pretended that the people with whom they ministered in previous generations were still the people they could reach in the future.

Rather than simply deal with our subjective impressions of the community, we wanted to know who was actually in our ministry area. What age groups are represented? What socioeconomic factors are shaping our community? Who are the unchurched people around us? What are the predicted population trends for the future? We formed a group that would gather all of the available demographic information to answer those questions. Some of their information surprised us. Some of it confirmed our assumptions. All of it began to energize our leaders with a passion to draw uncommitted people into a relationship with Jesus Christ.

Vision Questions:
How well do you know your neighborhood?
Who are the people in your ministry area with whom you are called to be in ministry?
How will the changing demographics of your community change the ministry of your church?

Vision Step 3: Observation

In their book, *How to Change Your Church Without Killing It*, Alan Nelson and Gene Appel point out that most ideas for change result from the observation of someone else's success. "Seeing or hearing of others who are doing well in ministry often motivates an effort to replicate the success" (p. 54).

Early on, I discovered that people in South Tampa didn't get out much. My guess is that it's probably true of most church folks. We tend to become so faithfully involved in our own congregation that we never see what other churches are doing. In order to stretch the thinking and experience of our leaders, we scheduled "best practice" visits to growing congregations who had something in common with our own church. Members of our task force participated in worship and met with the pastor and lay leadership in each congregation. The visiting teams then shared their observations with the rest of the task force.

In every visit, members of our teams discovered things that surprised and challenged them in thinking about our own ministry. One longtime member came back from a visit saying, "I noticed how bright their sanctuary was. I never realized how dark and dingy ours has become." Another person said, "Everywhere we go people are asking me about our mission. I guess it's time we get one!" I suspect that nothing else we did energized our leaders for mission more than these visits. We have continued to send our program staff and lay leadership to conferences at Willow Creek Community Church, Ginghamsburg United Methodist Church, and Church United Methodist in Fort Lauderdale to continue observing new models of ministry.

Vision Questions:
Do the leaders of your church get out much these days? Are they seeing the new things God is doing in growing congregations?

Vision Step 4: Listening

In describing the core ideology of effective corporations, Collins and Porras said, "They articulated what was inside them—what was in their gut, what was bone deep. It was as natural to them as breathing . . . the key word is *authenticity*. No artificial flavors. No added sweeteners. Just 100 percent genuine authenticity" (*Built to Last*, p. 76).

One of the goals for the task force was to listen for the authentic voice of the congregation and to enable our people to listen to each other. To accomplish that purpose, we developed a discussion guide for small groups that combined reflection on New Testament images of the church with opportunities for people to share the things that brought them to Hyde Park, the things that were most important to them, the things they thought needed to be changed, and their hopes for the future. A printed questionnaire led people through the process and provided a way for everyone to write their comments, whether they spoke them or not. Every member and friend of the congregation was invited to a neighborhood gathering in a church member's home. These were led by task force members who also took notes on the conversations to share with the rest of the task force.

The same discussion guide was used in just about every group of people in the congregation including Sunday school classes, youth groups, administrative committees, men's and women's ministry groups, and choirs. The more people sharing information the better! These gatherings provided an opportunity for every person to be heard, and built credibility in the

> *Vision Questions:*
> *How well are you listening to your people?*
> *How well are they listening to each other?*
> *What is the level of authenticity in your congregation?*
> *How could you create settings in which people could listen to each other and listen for an authentic word from the Spirit of God?*

process. They provided the task force with critically important information about the congregation. Listening to each other in these groups enlarged the participants' understanding of the diversity of perspectives within the congregation and built a sense of community around the visioning process. There's no question in my mind that for the congregation as a whole, this was the single most important element in the process.

Vision Step 5: Dialogue

It became very clear that the task force would not rush to any conclusions but would provide a setting in which a representative group of church members could enter into honest, open, heartfelt dialogue about what they were learning and hearing. In its best moments, that is precisely what happened. Sometimes members strongly disagreed with each other, but we were generally able to deal with those differences in a gracious and loving way. At our best, the goal was not to "win" our argument but to search for common understanding. As time went on and our discussions became more focused, the differences in the congregation were clearly mirrored in the task force itself.

> *Vision Questions:*
> *Can your leadership team enter into honest dialogue about the future of your church?*
> *Are your congregation's leaders willing and able to "speak the truth in love"?*

Vision Step 6: Prayer

I wish I could say that this task force had started out as intentional about its prayer life as we would eventually become. We were closer, I suspect, to the typical church group that opens with prayer and closes with prayer but functions between the prayers in about the same way as any civic group. But within the congregation and among the task force members were persons of great spiritual depth who were consistently holding the process in persistent prayer. The longer we worked together, the deeper the sense of spiritual community became. We experienced the kind of Christian community in which new visions could be born.

> *Vision Questions:*
> *How is your prayer life?*
> *How is the prayer life of your congregation?*
> *How long has it been since the leaders of your church have talked together about the disciplines of prayer?*
> *How long has it been since they prayed?*

Vision Step 7: Shared Information

Most church leaders grossly underestimate how difficult it can be to get information out to their congregation. The converse is that most church leaders overestimate the level of understanding within their congregation. Because so much power had been concentrated in so few people in our congregation, it was critically important for us to find as many ways as possible to share information about what was going on and to invite everyone to be a part of the process. The key word is "redundancy."

To underscore the openness of the process, the task force reported on their progress to every meeting of the administrative board. We encouraged church leaders to share information with their classes, small groups and committees. We printed regular updates in the church newsletter, always inviting feedback from the readers. Periodically, the chairperson or lay leader would share a word about the

> *Vision Questions:*
> *How well does information flow in your congregation?*
> *Does everyone have the opportunity to become a part of the conversation?*
> *How many different ways can you create redundant communication?*

process as a witness in worship. This continued openness to the congregation ensured that the mission and vision would not simply be the work of the task force, but would genuinely grow out of the body as a whole.

The Old Testament prophet heard the Lord say, "there is still a vision for the appointed time. . . . If it seems to tarry, wait for it; it will surely come, it will not delay" (Habakkuk 2:3). And so we waited as the process rolled on and on and on. No one could ever say that we rushed to a conclusion! There were times when the more impatient folks among us (including the preacher!) thought it was laboriously slow. But the reality is that it takes time for a new vision to ferment within the life of a congregation, particularly a long-established one. It takes time for people to become accustomed to the reasons for and possibilities of change. Rushing the process is like trying to rush a butterfly out of the cocoon. The vision has to emerge in its own time.

Finally, we began to put into words the mission and vision that the Spirit was shaping within us. We studied mission statements from other churches, picking up anything that resonated with members of the group and seemed to reflect what we had learned and heard. Many of the mission statements from other congregations were amazingly concise, causing one member of the task force to say, "We need more words!" He was convinced that because of the differences within the congregation, it would be easy to make false assumptions if the language were too general or vague. That's when two things happened.

First, some of our more theologically rigid members began to see that what was emerging would probably not fit into the narrow confines of their fundamentalist perspective. Some were disappointed that we would obviously continue to identify ourselves as a United Methodist congregation. Some protested. Some left. A few began to rethink their theological assumptions.

Second, the Spirit moved. The process had clearly bogged down. None of us seemed to be able to get a handle on what we needed to say. As we made our way through Lent, a sense of frustration about the process was growing.

Then Easter came. On Monday morning, the scent of lilies was still lingering in the sanctuary and Handel's "Hallelujah!" was still echoing in my soul. In my early morning time of prayer, I began asking God to break through the process and give us a clear direction. As I prayed, I began to sense a sentence taking form in my mind. I turned to the computer and began to type, still keeping centered in an attitude of prayer. I even tried typing with my eyes closed. I thought it would help maintain a spirit of prayer, but found it wasn't very effective. As I typed, a mission statement began to take form. When I felt that the prayer was ended, I stopped typing and read back across the words on the screen. I felt like the guy who said, "Eureka! I've found it!" The rough draft on the screen drew together all the major ideas the task force had been discussing. It was one of those times when I thought I might have experienced what the Bible means by inspiration.

When the task force met that week, I shared the draft with them. They talked about it, made several improvements in it, and suggested that we start testing it on the congregation. We made the rounds again, taking the draft copy to Sunday school classes, study groups, and committees for their discussion and input. We printed it in the newsletter and invited the congregation to comment on it. The task force discussed all of the suggestions we received and worked many of them into the statement. But for the most part, the congregational discussion of the draft confirmed that the words I had received on that Easter Monday morning were the authentic expression of God's mission and vision for us. So, here it is.

Our Mission

Hyde Park United Methodist Church is a community of people committed to Jesus Christ, empowered by the Holy Spirit, united in the love of God, and called to make that love real to others, through

*worship that glorifies God, celebrates our faith, and invites others to faith in Christ,

educational opportunities *that enable people to grow as faithful disciples and equip them for ministry in the world,*

caring relationships *that share the love of Christ,*

ministries of witness and service *that fulfill Christ's mission in our city and throughout the world.*

Our Vision

**A major, metropolitan congregation*

**primarily composed of people from the south Tampa peninsula, but drawing people from the larger metropolitan area because they find here a unique and exciting expression of Christian faith, community, ministry, and outreach*

**intentionally becoming a socially, economically, and racially inclusive congregation that bears witness to the wholeness of the kingdom of God,*

**clearly offering an expression of the Christian faith that is at the center of the Methodist tradition, which is:*

Christ-centered: *focused on the life, words, way, and Spirit of Jesus proclaimed in the gospel;*

biblically rooted: *encouraging spiritually alive, faithful study of the Bible, using tools of devotion and scholarship that are appropriate to a diverse body of people;*

warm-hearted: *a joyful, loving, laughing congregation that experiences the grace of God in Jesus Christ in personal and positive ways;*

*open-minded: a place where people search, think, question, and honestly express their growing experience of the faith in an accepting and affirming atmosphere;

*mission-directed: continuing the strong sense of mission that has been a part of our identity, both in terms of mission to the city and mission in the world;

*connectionally committed: as a part of the United Methodist Church, we will see ourselves as a leader/supporter of the connectional ministries in which we share.

Even as I typed the words into this manuscript, I felt the excitement that grew within the task force as we discussed, prayed, and worked our way through the meaning of the words. Having walked back through the factors that led us to it, I continue to be amazed at how authentically it spoke to the realities we were facing at the time. Having lived within it for nearly a decade, I still experience it as a living word from the Spirit that continues to lead us into the future. It was the fulfillment of the prophetic promise that by the creative power of the Holy Spirit, young people would see visions and old people would dream new dreams. (The biblical and theological content of the vision statements became major contributions to my book *Journey to the Center of the Faith*, published by Abingdon Press in 2001.)

The mission statement fulfilled the hopes of the task force member who said, "We need more words!" It offered a clear definition of who we believe God has called us to be. The only problem was that it was too wordy to remember. It was so complete that it would not be portable enough to carry around. That's when the Spirit spoke again. As is often the case in scripture, the Spirit spoke through one of the least likely characters.

The Spirit spoke through a simple, Southern lady with a simple, Southern way of expressing her faith. The truth is that most of the discussion and debate about the mission statement seemed to sail right over her head. We were engaged in a rather intense group discussion one day when she spoke up with innocence laced with frustration. "I don't know why y'all are workin' so hard at this," she said. "Why don't we just say we're supposed to share the love of Jesus?"

I'll confess that at first I was frustrated by the simplicity of her response and wondered why she didn't get it. But then I remembered the way the Wesleys centered the whole of the Christian faith in the love of God revealed in Christ. Looking back across the mission statement, the phrase popped out as never before: *"called to make that love real to others."* I pointed the words out to the group and they said, "That's it! We're here to make God's love real!" And so it was born. The whole meaning of the mission statement was contained in one simple phrase that has become the heart of our life together: *"Making God's Love Real."* We are called to be a community of people through whom the love of God that became a tangible reality in Jesus Christ becomes a tangible reality in the world.

After eighteen months of prayer, study, listening, and discussion, we were ready to invite the Church Conference to confirm the mission and vision that had been emerging through the process. Again, the information was shared throughout the congregation. For several weeks preceding the Church Conference, I preached on the key elements of the statement, laying a biblical and spiritual foundation for it and rooting in firmly in the spiritual history of our congregation. Finally, the day came for the Church Conference. About 200 people showed up, far beyond the normal attendance for this type of meeting. The presentation was made. When the vote was taken, it was nearly unanimous and everyone stood up in spontaneous applause. It was an unexpected expression of corporate joy in claiming the call of God that had planted in the hearts of the people.

I have no idea how the fresh vision of the Spirit might be born in your congregation. God's vision for Ginghamsburg United Methodist Church came to Michael Slaughter after he spent a day in an open field in prayer. God's vision for Christ Church, Fort Lauderdale, came to Dick Wills during a week of solitude, fasting, and prayer. Our vision emerged out of a community that wrestled with its identity and mission. The same Spirit who brooded over chaos and brought forth creation in Genesis, will bring new creation in ways that are uniquely designed for each congregation. The critical factor is not *how* it happens, but *that* it happens and that it happens for your congregation!

- How clear is God's vision for your congregation? Do you know where you are going? Has your congregation experienced something like the vision Peter announced on Pentecost?
- How would your congregation answer these questions?
  Who are we?
  Why are we here?
  What do we believe?
  Who are the people in our community who are not currently committed to Jesus Christ and what would it take for us to reach them?
  What is the unique ministry to which God is calling us in this community?
- Does your church's mission and vision express the authentic voice of your people?
- Are you willing to allow the vision to come in its own time?
- What steps will you take to discover the new vision that God is planting in the heart of your congregation?

CHAPTER 7

Finding Your Future in Your Past

Can we create a future worthy of our past?
—Lovett Weems, *Leadership in the Wesleyan Spirit*

It's not in the Bible, but tradition tells us that Jesus grew up in the home of a carpenter. That may explain the source of one of his most memorable parables. Jesus said there are two kinds of builders: a wise builder and a foolish builder. The wise builder built his house on the rock. The foolish builder built his house on the sand. Jesus said the rains fell, the floods came, the winds blew, and the house of the wise builder stood while the house of the foolish builder collapsed.

There is, of course, a secular version of that parable. It enlarges the original to include three builders. One built with straw, one with sticks, and one with bricks. This version took a slightly more violent spin by introducing a big, bad wolf who huffs and puffs and tries to blow the houses down. As you already know, the house of straw and the house of sticks fell while the house of bricks continued to stand and two out of three of the builders were at high risk of becoming pork chops.

Jesus didn't tell it quite that way, but he did say that anyone who hears his words and does them is a wise builder, and anyone who hears his words and does not do them is a foolish builder. One builder's house withstands the storms of change and the other's house doesn't. And the parable forces the question upon us: What kind of builder are you?

The parable applies to organizations and congregations just as surely as it applies to individuals. One of the most important lessons I learned in starting a new church was to be very careful about what we built into the early foundations of that congregation. The early values, beliefs, convictions, and attitudes become so deeply ingrained in the heart of a congregation that they never really go away. They become a part of the genetic code that continues to influence the life of the church for generations to come.

When I was appointed to Hyde Park, the congregation had been on that corner for ninety-three years. Like the wise pig's house, the sanctuary had been built of bricks in 1907. It withstood the rains and winds of the Florida hurricanes and an occasional flood in the basement of the 1922 vintage education building. (Though there is no historical data to support it, the local legend is that a Yankee church architect came to Tampa and convinced them to build with a basement just three blocks from the Hillsborough Bay!) In 1953–54 they gutted the sanctuary to redesign it for a new generation of growth and ministry. At the time of this writing, we are gutting it again, but the foundations, the roof, and three of the exterior walls will remain.

The stability of the sanctuary is an outward and visible sign of the inward and spiritual strength of the congregation. They've been there through good times and bad, in times of exciting growth and in times when folks wondered if the doors would have to be closed. It was immediately clear to me that any transformation for our future needed to be rooted in our past. The new life that would flow through the veins and arteries of our congregational body would come from the same spiritual heart that had been beating there for generations.

That you have made it this far through this book would indicate that you sense the call of God to engage in transformational leadership that will enable your congregation to become all that God intends for it to be in ministry to the world. It also suggests that you are a leader in a congregation that has spiritual roots in the past. Your church has a history. One of the surefire ways to short-circuit the transforming work of the Holy Spirit is to neglect that history and ignore that past. The terrain of church life in America today is littered with the remains of well-intended, Spirit-energized visions that crashed and burned because they failed to seriously consider the history and traditions of the congregation.

> *Lay claim to everything in your congregation's past that can be a positive influence for its future, and never stop telling the stories. Shape your vision of the future in ways that are consistent with the best in your past. Use the stories of what God has done in your history to frame your vision of the future.*

Let's face it: Every long-established church has some skeletons in the closet. The best thing I know to do is to lock the closet door and let them turn into dust. Paul said that he was "forgetting what lies behind and straining forward to what lies ahead" (Philippians 3:13). Unless the negative stuff from the past stands as a primary roadblock to God's vision for the future, I'd take Jesus' advice and "Let the dead bury their own dead; but as for you, go and proclaim the kingdom of God" (Luke 9:60). I would rather put energy into living into the future than fight with the past.

Some years ago I was invited to lead a visioning workshop for a congregation in a medium-sized Florida town that had two United Methodist churches within a few blocks of each other. I knew that prior to the denominational merger in 1939, one had been The Methodist Episcopal Church (the "Northern" Methodists) and the other had been The Methodist Episcopal Church, South. I was amazed to discover that ancient history was still a current reality

> *How well do you know the factors that gave birth to your congregation? How do those factors continue to influence your congregation today?*

in the hearts of many of the church leaders. After a day of trying to help them work through their past, I simply said, "You've got to get over this! Don't you realize that this city is packed full of people who couldn't care less about 1939 but who are really searching for the new life in Christ that you could offer?"

As I immersed myself in the history of our congregation, several specific stories from the past became the lens through which to see our future. I keep thinking that people will tire of hearing them, but every time I repeat them, the old-timers are reassured that this is still the church they have always known and rootless new-comers feel that they have become part of the ongoing work of the Spirit in this place.

The church history says that our church was born because the drawbridge that crossed the Hillsborough River would get stuck and Methodist families who lived in the newly developing Hyde Park neighborhood would be unable to get downtown to First Church. In March, 1899, they started a Sunday school for children in an old schoolhouse that sat on the corner where the sanctuary now sits. Twelve children and adults gathered for the first time and they sang, "I love to tell the story of Jesus and his love." At the beginning there was no ordained minister, just a group of Methodist laypeople who wanted to share the love of Jesus with the children and families who were moving into their neighborhood.

The preachers who read this book can probably see the homiletical train coming down the track! Hyde Park was born out of a passionate desire to share the love of God with people who have yet to experience it. We began as a church that cares about children and have been willing to do whatever necessary to accomplish that mission. And we have been a church that fulfills its mission through committed laypersons who take responsibility for ministry in their community.

The church history also records that when the Methodist Episcopal Church, the Methodist Episcopal Church, South, and the Methodist Protestant Church merged to create The Methodist Church in 1939, the uniting Conference for Florida was held at Hyde Park. Those divisions in Methodism went back to the Civil War when the church split, North and South, over the issue of slavery. But when they came back together, they came to Hyde

Park. Our history tells us that we are a church that unites divided people, a church where people of differing convictions are drawn together around the love of God in Christ.

There is the story of the renovation of the sanctuary in 1953–54. There are still people in the congregation who remember it. With the leadership of the Reverend Dr. Laurie Ray, who had served the church longer than any other pastor in its history—until I broke his record in 2003!—they gutted the 1907 structure down to the dirt and totally redesigned it. It was a bold thing to do, but it speaks of a congregation that is willing to change whatever is necessary to continue to grow and to be more effective in their ministry. I can assure you that our congregation has heard that story over and over again as we have moved into a building program that is renovating, tearing down, or building new structures on every inch of our property!

There is one story that does not appear in the published church history but continues to influence the way we live. In 1954 the congregation was preparing to move into their newly constructed fellowship hall and chapel. Tampa, like every old, Southern city, was experiencing the tension of the Civil Rights movement. We have found carbon paper copies of some rather heated letters that were written to the bishop of the Methodist Church in Florida by a church member who was also a prominent leader in the city, criticizing the church for speaking out in support of integration. The issue came home to Hyde Park in a meeting of the official board when a motion was made that was clearly intended to put the church on the side of segregation. In the debate that followed Dr. Ray said the motion was out of order because it was inconsistent with the gospel and with the order of the Methodist Church. A woman in the meeting said that this is God's church, not ours, and that we had no business trying to decide who could come in and who could not. When the vote was taken, the motion was defeated. I have recently learned that the reason we cannot find the record of the debate is that at the end of the meeting, the motion was made that the entire item be deleted from the minutes.

That one decision did not resolve all the issues of racism and we still have serious work to do to fulfill the inclusive vision of the kingdom of God. But at a decisive moment in its history, Hyde Park Church passed its exams on one of the most critical issues in our nation. We've been living out of the vision of that moment ever since. In fact, that event planted a vision of racial justice in the soul of a teenager named J. Lawrence McCleskey, who now tells the story as a bishop in the United Methodist Church.

I share these stories as examples of the way new life for the future can be rooted in the past. One of the important tasks of leadership is to affirm the best moments in a congregation's history as we reshape its life for the future. When people ask me to explain the amazing work that God is doing in our congregation, I always say that what we are seeing today grows directly out of the spiritual roots that were planted here more than a century ago.

"Use your congregation's history as a resource for change, to explore together your past and to weave these facts, events, and stories together to explain the present and open new options for the future. Have fun." Carl S. Dudley and Nancy T. Ammerman (Congregations in Transition, *quoted in* The Christian Century, *July 31-August 13, 2002, p. 29)*

The past became the present for us in a miraculous way in the summer of 2001. While we were finalizing the plans for the renovation of the sanctuary, we came upon what felt like a dead-end street. We simply could not find a way to resolve some of the issues before us. We scheduled a meeting of the Facilities Task Force to pray and reflect on what we should do.

On the morning of that meeting, in a moment not unlike the Easter Monday story I shared in the previous chapter, our church administrator was cleaning out some closets and discovered an old reel-to-reel tape recording. The label on the box identified it as the "Reconstitution of the Sanctuary" in 1954. No one even knew that it existed. She immediately found someone who could transfer the recording to a CD.

At the task force meeting that evening, we heard the voice of Dr. Laurie Ray placing the cornerstone in the renovated sanctuary. Two members of the current task force were specifically mentioned on the recording. The litany of dedication that day resonated with who we are becoming today. They prayed:

- For a church of which Jesus Christ is the chief cornerstone.
- For a church which will exalt not a religion of creed or authority, but a religion of saving grace, personal experience, and spiritual power.
- For a church that shall exalt the ministry of the open Bible.
- For a church that shall fulfill a ministry of social service and be a renewing and cleansing power in the community.
- For a church with an open door for all people rich or poor, homeless or destitute, who need the help of God through us.
- For a church that shall gather the children up in its arms and hold them close to Christ that they may grow up in the church and never be lost from the fold.
- For a church that shall stand for the truth that it is more blessed to give than to receive.

There were people in the congregation that day in 1954 who had been present for the laying of the original cornerstone in 1907. In that amazing moment, we felt a spiritual connection that took us all the way back to the founding of the church. As they placed the cornerstone in the wall, they prayed "for all who may share this spiritual adventure and with hope for all who shall worship in this house in years to come." We heard them praying for us. And in that meeting, when a new, unexpected option emerged that would became the solution to our problems, we knew that it was the answer to their prayers.

> *How can you make a direct link between what God did in your church in the past and what God is doing today?*

83

Linking our future with our past goes beyond telling the stories of our own congregational history. It also means digging farther back into the deep wells of our spiritual and theological traditions. A biblical model could be the story recorded in Genesis 26 where we learn that the Philistines had "stopped up and filled with earth" the wells that had been dug a generation before in the days of Abraham. Isaac's task was to dig again "the wells of water that had been dug in the days of his father Abraham." And there, in the old wells of his father, he found a spring of fresh, clear, life-giving water (Genesis 26:15-22).

It's absolutely true that we live in a day when "brand loyalty" to a particular denomination is a thing of the past. It is, however, a mistake to draw the conclusion that spiritual and theological traditions are irrelevant. I would contend that in a rapidly changing, constantly mobile, and largely rootless population, a congregation that lives with a vibrant sense of its spiritual and theological heritage is offering exactly what many people most deeply long to find.

As I write this book, American movie-goers are packing theaters to see a low-budget "sleeper" film called *My Big Fat Greek Wedding*. My guess is that one of the reasons people are drawn to this film is the warm-hearted way it deals with common traditions in a very ordinary Greek family. For all its quirky, oddball humor, it touches a place in our hearts that appreciates the value of identity that is passed on from generation to generation.

The mainline churches have a unique opportunity to offer spiritually thirsty people fresh water from the springs of their spiritual and theological traditions if they are willing to dig through the institutional clutter to find the spiritual vitality that gave birth to their movements in the first place. Let me be very clear in saying that I do not mean that we need to teach or preach institutional loyalty or narrow-minded denominationalism. Rather, I mean we should claim the deep, rich spiritual water that flows through two millennia of Christian experience in a way that enriches the lives of people today.

In the process of transformation at Hyde Park, we have never hesitated to identify ourselves with the central core of the

Wesleyan tradition while also communicating that we are clear that the family tree of the Christian church is a lot larger than our particular branch of it. However, living out of that tradition shapes our ministry in several specific ways. It shapes our understanding and practice of the sacraments of Holy Communion and Baptism. It is at the core of our mission with its emphasis on the love of God. It comes through clearly in our vision when we define ourselves as being "warmhearted," "open-minded," and "connectionally committed." It influences our worship in the way we follow the liturgical seasons. It provides the theological foundation out of which we select study resources. It underlies our organizational structure. It becomes the channel through which we share in global mission. We are very clear that our first priority is to make disciples, not to make United Methodists. But we are equally clear that our understanding and practice of discipleship is shaped by the Wesleyan roots out of which we have come.

We've also been very intentional about reaching into the deeper wells of the long history of Christian tradition. In our worship life, for instance, one of the specific goals in launching our contemporary worship service was to continue to maintain the liturgical tradition in fresh, contemporary forms. Our plans for a "Gen-X" ministry are based on an "ancient-future" approach that will combine ancient liturgical traditions with contemporary technology and music.

When I came to Hyde Park, I discovered that the congregation did not celebrate All Saints Day. Although John Wesley described All Saints as a day he particularly loved, the tradition goes back much farther than the eighteenth century. We immediately began celebrating the first Sunday in November as All Saints Sunday with a service in which we name all the members of our church who died in the previous year. The worship team has continued to develop the service so that it has become one of the most meaningful worship experiences of our church year. Each year we find fresh ways of interpreting this ancient tradition for our life together. The same has been true for celebrating the Baptism of our Lord (the first Sunday after Epiphany) with the renewal of baptismal vows, Ash Wednesday with the imposition of ashes, and Good Friday with the ancient tradition of Tenebrae. Every year people who have been previously unchurched or who never experienced these traditions share with us how meaningful these services are for them. By digging in old wells, they have found fresh water to quench the thirst of their souls.

Here's my bottom line. Two thousand years of Christian tradition should have taught us something! By connecting people with the long flow of spiritual life in the church, we discover who we are in the present on the basis of who we have been in the past. To abandon or ignore the long spiritual traditions in which we stand is as arrogant as it is foolish.

> *How is your congregation appropriating the spiritual traditions out of which it has come?*
>
> *Is your congregation helping people discover the rich resources of spiritual discipline and ministry that they have inherited in the Body of Christ?*

One of the divine ironies in the Hyde Park story is that the members who have been around the longest are the ones who are the most excited about the future. When the Church Conference was called to approve the master plan for the redesign and renovation of our facilities, several of them said, "Let's get on with this. We want to see this completed before we die!" I'm convinced that their excitement about the most radical changes in the history of their church grows out of positive answers to four questions.

First, are people's hearts right? Resistance to change has very little to do with age and everything to do with the heart. The folks I've described are tenderhearted people who are constantly growing in their relationship with Christ. They live with a burning passion to "tell the old, old story of Jesus and his love." It's possible for people of any age to become hard-hearted, mean, cantankerous grouches. About all I know to do for them is to keep praying that God will heal their damaged hearts while not allowing them to undermine the movement of the Spirit by their meanness. But when their hearts are right, mature Christian people love sharing the love of Jesus more than they love their past. The heart of the matter is always a matter of the heart.

Second, do they believe in the mission? Because they were fully engaged in the mission and vision process, they can see how the changes we are making will help their church be more effective in reaching the next generation for Christ. They really care about children who are growing up in this culture and want their church to make a positive difference in those children's lives. They are more deeply committed to the mission than to the method.

Third, do they feel secure? We provided a sense of security for people in knowing that the leadership of the congregation valued the past and that the church we are becoming today is consistent with the church we have been. People can see that the changes we are undergoing grow out of the spiritual taproot of the church's life and history.

Fourth, do they still have their place? As we have added new, contemporary services, we have been very careful to maintain high-quality traditional worship. We have continued to follow the traditional seasons of the liturgical year in all of our services and to celebrate the sacraments using the United Methodist liturgy. We've tried to draw direct connections with our Methodist history and traditions. We picked up a little-known paragraph in our *Book of Discipline* that enables a Church Conference to elect honorary members as a way of celebrating the long-term ministry of our older members. It has been a way of affirming and celebrating our history. When we relocated the adult Sunday school classes, we made sure that the class with the older members still had their familiar chairs! In large ways and small, we have celebrated and affirmed our past even as we have been redesigning our ministry for the future.

In August 2001, we held the last worship service in the old sanctuary. We knew that we would not be back for at least eighteen months and that when we returned we would enter a very different place. We also knew that the last worship service would be a profoundly moving and important moment in which to celebrate our past and claim our future. We invited the oldest former pastor to return to lead us in prayer. We recognized everyone who had been baptized, confirmed, or married in the building. We gave thanks for all God had done in the lives of people within those walls. Then we affirmed the vision that is before us. At the conclusion of the service, we processed out of the building carrying the symbols of our worship: the Bible, candles, baptismal water, communion chalice, and altar paraments. Row by row, the congregation followed, many with tears in their eyes, as we made our way into the activities center where we would worship during the renovation.

In the week prior to that service, I received an email message from a person whose family had been sitting in the same pew for three generations. Here's what the family member wrote.

> While I don't sit in that second pew from the front much anymore, I plan to sit there with my family at 11:00 this Sunday morning. It's hard not to be sentimental about that old pew. I have shared many happy and sad times there, all of which I am grateful to have had in that pew in that church to provide me with the peace to experience it all. While I don't believe in dwelling on the past, I do believe the past shapes us, molds us, and prepares us to move into the future. Maybe it is symbolic that we are turning the sanctuary around. For now the memories will be behind us as we sit in the newly renovated sanctuary and the future memories will be before us. I don't know where that old pew will wind up, but wherever I sit, I know I will continue to find the peace to experience whatever lies ahead.

When it comes down to it, there are only two kinds of builders in this world. There are wise builders and there are foolish builders. Wise builders build on solid foundations from the past. Foolish builders act as if nothing happened before they came on the scene. When the storms of change come, the house of the wise builder will stand and the house of the foolish builder will fall. Jesus forces the question upon us: Which kind of builder are you?

- How well do you know the spiritual history of your congregation? How long has it been since you listened to the stories from the past?

- What can you find in your church's past that can become a foundation for the future? How can you envision the work of God in the present growing out of what God has done in your church in the past?
- Whose voices from the past might become the voice of the Spirit for your present?

CHAPTER 8

Prayer That Makes a Difference

*History belongs to the intercessors, who believe the future into being.
. . . The future belongs to whoever can envision . . . a new and
desirable possibility, which faith then fixes upon as inevitable.*
—Walter Wink, *Engaging the Powers*

When people ask me to name the most important single element in the transformation process, I always say the same thing. We're learning to pray. We're continuing to discover what it means to live and lead out of a life of prayer. Prayer is the means by which we feel the pulse of the Spirit of God at work within and through our life together.

Lovett Weems records a penetrating question from the *Large Minutes* in the early years of Methodism. The question was: "Why are we not more holy?" The answer was that people were "looking for the end, without using the means" (*Leadership in the Wesleyan Spirit*, p. 120). Our experience has convinced us that the primary means by which God removes the heart of stone and gives us a heart of flesh is disciplined, listening, obedient prayer.

Just about every church I know talks about prayer. To one degree or another, most churches practice it. But if your experience is like mine, you've attended more than your share of church meetings that "opened" with a prayer and "closed" with a prayer but nothing that happened between the prayers would have been any different if it had been a meeting of a civic organization or a corporate board. Even worse, many of us have found ourselves in settings where the tools of prayer are used as a subtle form of manipulation to get a group to do what the leader had already decided needed to be done. All too often in the church, what we actually do and how we do it do not indicate that we expect the God to whom we pray to become an active participant in the process. Nor is there much practical evidence that we, in our human imperfection and weakness, can feel, sense, and know the active leadership of the Holy Spirit in our decision making. We offer a polite nod, a tip of the hat to God, but we act as if we are called to make decisions on our own with God sitting on the sidelines, waiting to be asked to "bless" what we have decided to do.

It's not that we don't believe in God. We do! But we work as if the church is the place where we do something for God, not the place where God does something for, in, and through us. We debate issues, make the best decisions we can, and ask God to bless what we have decided to do, rather than expect God to direct us in doing what God wants done through us.

Finally, however, the day comes when our best human wisdom is not enough to get us through, our human stamina is not enough to keep us going, and our best attempts at being faithful are utterly inadequate for the task. In those times, I've often found myself drawn back in helpless exhaustion to the words of the psalmist:

> Unless the LORD builds the house,
>   those who build it labor in vain. . . .
> It is in vain that you rise up early
>   and go late to rest,
> eating the bread of anxious toil;
>   for he gives sleep to his beloved. (Psalm 127:1-2)

Did you hear the story about the guy who got the first permit to open a tavern in a small, country town? The church folks were so upset they called a prayer meeting to ask God to intervene. A few days later, lightning hit the tavern and burned it to the ground. The church folks were outwardly surprised and inwardly pleased until they received word that the tavern owner was suing them. He claimed their prayers were responsible for the fire that destroyed the tavern. The church folks hired an attorney who drafted a strongly worded deposition to deny the charge. The judge listened to both sides and then said, "I'm not sure how I will rule on this case, but based on the testimony today, it appears that the tavern owner believes in prayer and the church folks don't."

> *Do you really believe that prayer is the means by which God's will is accomplished in our lives? Do you believe that it makes any difference to pray? Are your actions consistent with what you believe?*

When I thanked my cardiologist for saving my life, he told me to thank the people who prayed for my heart because he wasn't sure that what he did made much difference. I've never asked him to explain what he meant. I suppose it could have been one of those lighthearted things a doctor says when the patient is his pastor! But I think he meant it. I'm grateful for his knowledge and skills. God would have had a hard time healing me without them. But I know that the faithful, disciplined prayers of God's people became the means by which God's healing power was released in my body through or in spite of my physician.

In the same way, I am quite sure that the total of what has been happening around Hyde Park Church is far greater than the sum of the parts. Each person has made an essential contribution to the work, but the only explanation for the vitality, growth, and witness of this congregation is that the Spirit of God has taken our human resources and expanded them beyond our human capacity. This exponential expansion of our gifts happened through prayer.

Everyone who knew Esther would agree that she was one of the most unique characters in the recent history of Hyde Park Church. Always loyal, often outspoken, slightly cantankerous, and sometimes downright demanding, she also believed in prayer. She was a contemporary version of the central character in what is often called "the parable of the importunate widow." The word "importunate" doesn't appear in the text, but it means "asking repeatedly, annoyingly persistent." That's exactly what she was. Jesus said the judge finally gave her what she wanted "so that she may not wear me out by continually coming" (Luke 18:5). Years before I came on the scene, Esther gathered a few people together who met every Sunday morning to pray for their pastors and for the future of the church. With a certain lack of humility, she would remind me that I was appointed here because of her prayers. There were times when I didn't turn out to be the answer she wanted, but even when she didn't agree with what we were doing, I knew that her "importunate" prayers were still being lifted to God for her—and she did consider it "her"— church. I am pretty sure that the work of heart transformation that the Spirit has been doing among us continues to be the result of consistent, faithful prayer on the part of Esther and a host of other "importunate" folks like her. In fact, because I believe in the communion of saints, I can't help sensing that her prayers continue to be lifted for us around the heavenly throne.

> *Who are the people of "importunate" prayer in your congregation? How can you become a part of their life of prayer?*

The discipline of prayer patterned after the "importunate" widow began to shape the decision-making process within our congregation. It became a very practical reality as we prepared to launch an alternative worship service.

As a long-established congregation worshiping in an historically designated building in an historic district of the city, we did traditional worship very well. Our demographic research, however, confirmed that we would need to offer other worship alternatives to reach the unchurched population around us. For over a year, we studied, visited other churches, read books, listened to tapes, and discussed the possibilities before us. Out of that process we shaped the vision of what we were being called to. Then we ran into a major roadblock. We simply could not find musicians. We searched. We contacted the music departments in all the colleges and universities. We sent letters to our seminaries. We even considered "buying" musicians away from another congregation! But we simply could not find the right people. Finally, we decided to give up and pray. The committee stopped working so hard at it and began prayerfully waiting for God to lead.

Several years earlier, we had begun giving the Chancel Choir some time off in the month of August. In their place, we offered a "Summer Music Festival" that was intended to expose the congregation to a variety of musical styles for worship. One of our members, who leads the jazz music program at the University of South Florida, came each year to lead one of these summer services in jazz. In 1995 he asked if he could bring along an African American woman named Belinda Womack. I recognized her name as the top jazz vocalist in the Tampa Bay area, but I did not even know if she was a Christian.

Belinda brought along her children that morning. When the services were over, she told me that her children liked the Sunday school so much that they wanted to come back. When she showed up in the New Member Orientation Class, I told her I thought that God might have more here for her than just a new church home. When I told her that we had been planning a contemporary service for nearly two years, she said that for the past two years she had been looking for a church home and had been feeling drawn back to her gospel roots. Here's the story in her words.

Until July, 1995, my life was pretty "livable." I would sing with my band, on occasion conduct worship services, do community work, and work as a music teacher. I had felt God's call on my life back in 1989, but I ignored the voice. God allowed me to continue on my way, but his voice got louder and more commanding. I found myself participating in more church gigs. Then I received a call from Chuck Owen to sing at Hyde Park United Methodist Church. Satan knew that Chuck's invitation was the start of a new work in me that God had planned all along and he wasn't about to miss the opportunity to convince me to ignore God's call. After accepting Chuck's invitation, I searched for any reason to cancel. Ironically, nothing came up to allow me to bow out gracefully. I even brought my children knowing that they were not completely open to visiting yet another church, sitting in yet another unfamiliar Sunday school where more than likely they would be the only African American children there, enduring yet another "concert" with their mother and afterwards accepting gracefully mechanical "Thank yous" and "What sweet children" comments while drinking bad orange drink and eating cookies.

Surprisingly, God was about to set me on the very path that I had tried to avoid! To my astonishment, my children were more than accepting of the people who greeted us, fell in love with the Sunday school, didn't even notice that they were the only African American children present, thought the music was really cool as well as the preacher's sermon, and loved the fresh donuts, cheesy goldfish crackers, and cool orange juice that they were given. I, in turn, felt the tugs of God's call even louder in my ear. I began to explore becoming a member and joining the choir. Then one day I heard the loud voice of God say, "Got-cha!" Suddenly, I found myself in the midst of what would prove to be a wonderful transformation of my life's direction and work.

Looking back now, it's no longer a surprise to me that for at least two years, God had been preparing us for each other. The result has been one of the most amazing growth opportunities in the history of our church. At the time of this writing, we have two traditional and two contemporary services every Sunday morning, enabling us to reach a wider range of people than we have ever reached before. We are beginning the process of prayerful preparation for a new ministry for Gen-Xers and are trusting God to provide the leadership for it through the same process of prayer, just the way God provided in the past.

How have you seen God's Spirit preparing the way for new ministries in your church? Are you willing to wait for God to lead?

There's an old story about the Army chaplain who, in the heat of a ferocious battle, dove into a foxhole for cover. An instant later a frightened young soldier dove in beside him. When the young soldier saw the chaplain, he reached out, grabbed the cross on the chaplain's lapel and said, "Quick Padre! How do you work this thing?" Well, how does prayer work? What kind of prayer makes a difference? What kind of prayer is so rooted in the depths of Scripture that it might actually make some kind of difference in our lives?

In the eighteenth chapter of Luke's Gospel, Jesus tells two stories that offer a shocking word about the kind of prayer that makes a difference, not only in the life of the person who prays, but in the world for which that person prays. Those stories and our congregational experience lead me to several principles about living and leading in prayer.

1. Prayer that makes a difference is prayer that is aligned with the redemptive purpose of God.

A common theme in both the story of the praying widow and the story of the Pharisee and the tax collector is centered in the word "justice." Jesus described the widow crying out for justice from the judge. Jesus said that the tax collector was the man who went home justified that day.

When I hear the word "justify," my imagination goes to the print shop. Back in the days of moveable type, the printer would justify lines of type so that both margins were even and so that the letters between the two margins on each line were all in the right relationship to each other. The computer does all that for us automatically now, but it involves the same process. Biblically speaking, to justify is to bring everything into right relationship with the purpose of God. It is that sense of God's order of things that brings people into right relationship with each other and right relationship with God. In the larger sense, it describes God's redemptive work of bringing the whole creation into harmony with God's intention for it. Paul describes it as "a plan for the fullness of time, to gather up all things in [Christ], things in heaven and things on earth" (Ephesians 1:10).

Most of us know what New Testament theologian Walter Wink meant when he acknowledged that "we are not easily reduced to prayer" (*Engaging the Powers*, p. 297). He writes that people who pray do not do so because of their intellectual understanding of prayer, but because the struggle in which they are engaged demands it. Sooner or later, transformational leaders who are engaged in the process of congregational cardiology discover that the stress, conflict, and pain of change force them to move into a deeper place of prayer than they had known before. But even as they are driven into a deeper, more intimate experience of God's presence in prayer, the very act of praying draws them into a larger vision of God's redemptive purpose. Wink declares:

> Intercession, to be Christian, must be prayer for God's reign to come on earth. It must be prayer for the victory of God over disease, greed, oppression, and death in the concrete circumstances of people's lives, now. In our intercessions we fix our wills on the divine possibility latent in the present moment, and then find ourselves caught up in the whirlwind of God's struggle to actualize it. (*Engaging the Powers*, p. 303)

In a vibrant image of what a local congregation might become, Wink says that when we pray "we are engaged in an act of cocreation, in which one little sector of the universe rises up and becomes translucent, incandescent, a vibratory center of power that radiates the power of the universe" (*Engaging the Powers*, pp. 303-4).

We've discovered that prayer that makes a difference is aligned with the larger perspective of the way God's self-giving love in Christ brings all things into right relationship with the promise of God's kingdom coming on earth as it is fulfilled in heaven. Prayer is the process by which we bring our lives, our ministry, and our mission into proper relationship with the redemptive purpose of God revealed in Jesus Christ so that our life together becomes a translucent center of loving power for the transformation of the world. I'm convinced that one of my primary tasks in preaching is to continually lift up that large vision of God's purpose and to enable the congregation to see our part in it.

I can assure you that when I was gasping for air with congestive heart failure, most of my energy was focused on the immediacy of survival! In the same way, one of the greatest dangers for any church suffering from congregational cardiomyopathy is the natural tendency to focus on mere survival. When a congregation becomes aware that it is in or on the edge of decline, the primary question can easily become, "What can we do to help our church survive? How do we keep the doors open? How will we pay the bills?" But when survival becomes the primary motivation for change, the congregation will inevitably turn in on itself and become so centered in its survival needs that it will be ineffective in responding to the real needs of real people in the world around it. New people who come in contact with the congregation immediately sense that the church is not so much interested in using its resources to meet their need as it is interested in using them for its own survival. In the end, a focus on survival always becomes self-defeating. The process of dying and rising again, which is symbolized in our baptism, means letting go of our desire to do whatever we can do to simply survive.

One of the ways in which we have attempted to keep that larger vision before us is through continued attention to the global ministries of the church. In our new member orientation, we help people see that by becoming a part of the United Methodist Church, they will be immediately connected with people and ministries in every part of the world. In our congregational prayers, we boldly lift up the immediate needs of the world around us, whether that means praying for AIDS victims in Africa, politically oppressed people in South America, or the victims of conflict in the Middle East. In our annual "Mission Celebration," we bring in representatives of all of the mission agencies we support along with an outstanding speaker as a witness of the global ministry of the church. During the years that

> *Is your congregation asking "What must we do to survive?" or "What must we do to align ourselves with God's redemptive purpose for the world?" Is your life of prayer focused on meeting the survival needs of your congregation or on meeting the larger needs of a bruised, broken, and spiritually hungry world?*

we have been involved in a major building program, we have also enlarged our focus on the needs of the world around us.

Genuine, Christ-centered, biblically rooted prayer lifts our vision beyond the survival needs of our own congregation to see the way this particular congregation can become a part of God's redemptive purpose at work in the world. Praying the way Jesus taught us forces us to realign our ministries around the vision of God's kingdom coming on earth as it is already fulfilled in heaven.

2. Prayer that makes a difference is prayer that is persistent in seeking.

When I try to picture the "importunate widow" in Jesus' parable, I think of Ma Joad in John Steinbeck's classic, *The Grapes of Wrath,* who was absolutely determined to get the family through to California and to hold the family together in its most desperate hours. The woman in Jesus' parable was no polite, sweet little lady making a quilt or crocheting a doily. She could not afford to waste time on things that didn't matter. She was absolutely determined to get what she so desperately needed.

Jesus set the parable in the framework of gross inequity with the power and authority of the unjust judge on one side and the weakness and helplessness of the widow on the other. But this widow simply would not quit. She kept pounding on the judge's door, calling on his telephone, sending him email, pestering him day in and day out until finally, in sheer desperation, the unjust judge said, "Whew, I can't take this woman any longer! I'd better give her what she wants before she wears me out!"

Jesus was not saying that God is like that unjust judge. This is one of those "how much more parables." Jesus was saying that if this corrupt, unjust judge would respond to the persistence of this widow, then "how much more" will the infinitely just and all-loving God respond to those who with unwavering persistence call upon God?

When Jesus got to the punch line, he asked a question that was not directed to the judge or the widow, but was directed to the hearers of the story: "When the Son of Man comes, will he find faith on the earth?" (Luke 18:8). Will he find that "importunate" kind of persistence in prayer in us?

Biblical prayer is intense. It is profound. It is constantly moving toward deeper trust. It involves holding on to what we know to be the redemptive will and purpose of God until we see that purpose accomplished in our own lives and in the world in which we live. Prayer that makes a difference hangs on, holds on, and refuses to give in until God's kingdom has come and God's will has been done.

In very practical terms, persistence in prayer has meant that we have structured into our life together some basic patterns of spiritual discipline and prayer. Personally, I know that the quality of my spiritual leadership is in direct proportion to my discipline of daily meditation and prayer. In the same way, each program staff person is expected to develop his or her own personal discipline of prayer. As a ministry leadership team, the church staff meet together every Tuesday morning for worship and focused prayer for the needs of the congregation. We begin on Sunday morning by gathering before any of the activities of the day for a time of prayer in which laypersons pray for the worship leaders. Our Gathering of Adult Leaders underscores the importance of prayer for all of our small group and ministry team leaders. An Intercessory Prayer Ministry provides a structured format for at least one layperson to spend at least one hour every day in prayer for the needs of our congregation. The *Companions in Christ* program (available from Upper Room Ministries) is leading people

> *What's your persistence factor? Have you developed a pattern of persistent prayer within your life? Is that kind of persistent prayer a vital part of the life of your congregation?*

in developing deeper spiritual disciplines in their lives. In short, we are persistently at work to find practical ways of shaping our life together around our experience of prayer.

3. Prayer that makes a difference is prayer that is centered in the love and mercy of God.

In the second of these companion parables, Jesus again painted a scene with bold, contrasting colors. He set the story up by saying that a very good guy and a very bad guy both went up to the temple to pray. Immediately, the first hearers of this parable knew which was which. The Pharisee was the good guy. He was the one who did everything right, obeyed all the rules, and had good reason to stand in the temple and say, "God, I thank you that I am not like other people. I say my prayers everyday. I go to the synagogue. I tithe. God, I thank you that I am not like all the evil people in this world, particularly like this tax collector over here" (Luke 18:11-12, author paraphrase).

And the first hearers immediately picked out the bad guy in the parable. He was the tax collector. Tax collectors were corrupt. They were in cahoots with the occupation forces of Rome. They represented the worse effects of human greed. They were rejected by every faithful Jew. The tax collector was so bad, in fact, that the only thing he had any right to do was to stand in the corner, beating his breast and saying, "God, be merciful to me, a sinner!" (Luke 18:13).

There was no surprise in the parable yet. That's just what people would have expected each of them to say. The surprise came when Jesus pointed to the tax collector and said, "I tell you, this man went down to his home justified rather than the other; for all who exalt themselves will be humbled, but all who humble themselves will be exalted" (Luke 18:14). Talk about a surprise! Jesus' interpretation of the scene was a radical reversal of everything the people expected. By turning their expectations inside out and upside down, Jesus pointed toward the radical transformation that is at the very heart of the mercy of God.

Prayer that makes a difference lives with a humble awareness of our need of God's mercy. It grows out of a keen awareness that at our very best, we are incomplete, fallible human beings. At our highest, we fall short of the glory of God. Our best wisdom is incapable of comprehending all the complexity of life. Our greatest strengths are weak in comparison to the strength of God's redemptive purpose in the world. It's the kind of prayer that engages us in the process of transformation by which the self-giving love of God that was made real among us in Jesus becomes a tangible reality in and through our lives. It's the kind of praying that gives us a tender heart for people just like this tax collector. It's the kind of praying that enables us to love self-righteous people like that Pharisee, too.

We often hear people in our New Member Orientation Class say that Hyde Park was the church for which they had been searching for a long time. When we probe into those comments to find out exactly what it was that drew them into the congregation, the responses often point toward a gracious acceptance of people the way they are, a nonjudgmental spirit, a sense that people are loved and accepted as they are, that they don't need to put on some sort of artificial religious façade. If that's true—and I hope it is!—it is because we are learning to live with a heartfelt sense of our own need of God's mercy, which enables us to extend that mercy to others.

> *How tender is your heart? Are the leaders of your congregation learning to live with a humble awareness of their need of the mercy and grace of God? How effectively are they extending that mercy to others?*

So, what have we learned about living and leading out of that kind of prayer? And what are we doing to keep our congregational life centered in it?

In 1997 we broke ground for the largest construction project in the one-hundred-year history of Hyde Park Church. A few months into the project, the construction superintendent told our church administrator that he had learned by experience that if a project gets off to a good start, it usually goes well the whole way through. But if it gets off to a rocky start, he can usually expect to have problems all along the way. This one, he said, was off to a very good start. Then he said, "You know, it feels like there's something going on around here."

His comment became the starting point for a "state of the church" message that attempted to describe what God had been doing around Hyde Park, based on the description of prayer recorded in Psalm 40. First, the psalmist said, "I waited patiently for the LORD; / he inclined to me and heard my cry" (Psalm 40:1). We're learning to wait to make a decision until there is some common awareness that we have heard from the Lord.

As the word has spread about what God has been doing at Hyde Park, we've been receiving calls and visits from the pastors and lay leadership of other congregations around the state. One day our church administrator told me about a call she received from a friend of mine who is one of the outstanding laypersons in another historically strong congregation. Having been conditioned to think within the organizational structures by which United Methodists generally try to get things done, he wanted to know who makes the decisions around here. What boards, committees, or groups hold power and authority over others? He was surprised when she told him that we have reduced elected committees to the bare minimum and hardly ever vote on anything any more. Most decisions are made by concensus through prayer. When votes are taken, they are generally a means of giving formal expression to the sense of direction that the Spirit has already given. We're not yet where we want to be, and we still have a lot to learn, but we are

How are decisions made in your congregation? Are you learning to wait patiently for the Spirit of God to lead through prayer?

discovering what it means to wait patiently for the Spirit to show us the way.

Second, the psalmist said, "He drew me up from the desolate pit, / out of the miry bog, / and set my feet upon a rock, / making my steps secure" (Psalm 40:2).

It would be less than honest to give the impression that learning to live and lead through prayer is a smooth transition or that it always results in flawless fulfillment of our mission. Sometimes it's a lot more like sloshing through a miry bog, with every step slipping and sliding on wet clay. Time and time again we have come to swampy impasses where we could not seem to find a clear way to go. And each time, we have seen the Spirit of God set our feet on a rock and make our steps secure.

I previously described the process that led to the approval of our mission statement. When all of our study, discussion, debate, and prayer had seemed to reach a dead end, the Spirit moved in unexpected ways to give form and substance to the mission that God was forming in the heart of our life together. It happened again in launching the contemporary worship service. It happened

Where have you found yourself "in a miry bog"? How have your feet been set on a solid path through prayer?

again in the planning process for the building program. In large ways and small, God has set our feet on a rock and shown us the way through listening, patient, obedient prayer.

Third, the psalmist shouted, "[God] put a new song in my mouth, / a song of praise to our God" (Psalm 40:3).

There's not much question about it: the most obvious thing that has been going on around here is that God is teaching us to sing and praise God with new songs and in new ways. It goes right to the heart of our mission, which says that we provide worship which "invites others to faith in Christ." We've learned that if we are going to invite spiritually hungry, biblically illiterate, unchurched people to faith in Christ, we are going to have to learn to do it in language and rhythms that they can understand.

There is, of course, nothing new about that. That's how

> *How has God been giving you new songs to sing? How is your life of prayer making you more sensitive to the language and rhythm of the people you are called to reach?*

Methodism got its start. Back in the eighteenth century, John and Charles Wesley kept their roots in the Anglican tradition, but they put the message of God's love and grace into language the common people— people outside the walls of the church—could understand. They set their words to tunes that common people could actually sing. As a spiritual awakening, Methodism sang its way into the hearts and lives of people. The tune keeps changing while the message remains the same.

The result is that "many will see and fear, / and put their trust in the LORD" (Psalm 40:3).

The psalmist describes what God is doing around here. Often in the most amazing and unexpected ways, God is drawing some of the most unexpected people into our congregation. They have seen what's happening here, and they want to put their trust in the kind of God they experience in the lives of people in this congregation.

Dick Wills warns emerging spiritual leaders that it's dangerous to pray, as he did, that God would send to Christ Church the people that no one else wanted. "That is a dangerous prayer . . . because I know that God answers that prayer. All you have to do is look around the church I serve at all the new people who have come to faith. They are a really strange looking group of people. They are nothing like who I would have chosen to be a part of Christ Church" (*Waking to God's Dream*, p. 83).

I continue to remind our congregation that we are not here to relate people to the institutional church; we are here to relate people to Jesus Christ. We are not here to make people religious; we are here to make disciples of Jesus. We are not here to attempt to resolve all of the conflicted issues that divide people around the circumference of the Christian faith; we are here to draw people deeper and deeper into the central core of the Christian gospel, which is the love and grace of God in Jesus Christ. By keeping

> *Are you willing for God to send you the people no one else wants? Do you genuinely want God to draw new people into discipleship through your church?*

that focus clear, we are continuing to see all sorts of people come from all sorts of places to be drawn into the love of God in Christ.

Then the psalmist promised, "Happy are those who make / the LORD their trust" (Psalm 40:4). Another thing God has been doing in us through prayer may come as a surprise to people who have the impression that prayer is a deadly serious ordeal. Through our life of prayer, God has been teaching us to laugh. God is teaching us the genuine happiness that comes through obedience. God has enabled us to share the faith with great joy.

I suspect that one of the most common heart ailments in the church is a terminal seriousness. Too many church folks take themselves far too seriously. I keep reminding myself that G. K. Chesterton said that angels can fly because they take themselves so lightly. We are called to take the gospel and the needs of the world around us with utmost seriousness, while not taking ourselves seriously at all. A person who walks though the halls of our buildings on Sunday morning, visits any of our classes

> *Is your congregation discovering the joy that comes in obedience? What's the laughter quotient in your church?*

and groups on almost every night of the week, stands around in the courtyard or under the Welcome Center tent, or meets people in our Aldersgate Corner Bookstore and Coffee Shop is almost guaranteed to hear the sound of laughter. Not slushy, slurpy, artificially contrived stuff, but real, genuine, human laughter—the honest expression of great joy.

The psalmist concluded, "You have multiplied, O LORD my God, / your wondrous deeds" (Psalm 40:5).

One of the most amazing things I'm learning about the way God works through prayer is that God does not build the Kingdom by addition, but by multiplication. As God's people live and lead out of a life that is centered in God's presence through prayer, God's Spirit works in and through their lives to exponentially extend the love of God to others.

We have seen the way God multiplies our efforts in the way new people have been drawn into our congregation. We have seen God's exponential deeds in the multiplication of opportunities to offer ourselves in service to the community. And we have seen God's multiplication process at work in the financial stewardship of our people.

Across recent years, our stewardship program has moved away from funding the church's needs and toward meeting people's deep need for spiritual direction in ordering their financial lives around their commitment to Jesus Christ. Our growth in stewardship is not the result of creative fund-raising. Although we used professional consultants in funding our building program, the funding of the ongoing ministries of the church is the evidence of what happens when people orient their lives around their commitment to Jesus Christ. The love and compassion of God begins to flow in their lives, and out of that wellspring of love they respond by giving themselves to others.

As I look at the many signs of growth in our congregation, I cannot help singing with the psalmist, "You have multiplied, O LORD my God, / your wondrous deeds . . . / none can compare with you. / Were I to proclaim and tell of them, / they would be more than can be counted" (Psalm 40:5).

> *How would you count the ways in which God has multiplied the growth, life, and ministry of your congregation? How has that exponential growth been connected to your congregation's life of prayer?*

Finally, the psalmist points in the direction of our continuing desire to live and lead out of a life of prayer in asking for "an open ear" (Psalm 40:6). He offers himself to God when he prays, "Here I am . . . / I delight to do your will" (Psalm 40:7-8). Those two verses describe the way we intend to continue to grow in our life of prayer. First, we want to live with "an open ear" to whatever God has to say to us. Prayer is becoming more a process of listening for God's direction than it is asking for God's favors. And then, when we hear God's direction, we want to live in the kind of obedience that says, "Here I am!" and delights to do God's will.

The construction manager got it right: there is something going on around here. And what's going on around here is a direct result of learning to live and lead out of a life of prayer. The more we see God doing, the more we long for an open ear and for joyful obedience to God's will!

CHAPTER 9

The Heart of Transformation

What does the finished product look like?
And what is the process for making one?
—Adam Hamilton, *Leading Beyond the Walls*

It's one thing to have a mission; it's another thing to actually live it. Living it means aligning all of the congregation's resources to accomplish that mission. It means saying yes to everything that contributes to it. Even harder, it means saying no to a multitude of good things that do not contribute directly to the mission. We've been learning that God has many good things to be done in this world that, because they are not directly aligned with our mission, are not tasks to which God is calling us. In order to gain more clarity about those issues, we began searching for the answers to some deeper questions:

- How does this mission become a transforming reality in the lives of real people?
- What is the definable process by which the Spirit is at work to accomplish the mission of this church through the lives of our people?

Through more prayer, study, and reflection, we came to this answer. "Making God's Love Real" means that we are in the business of "transforming ordinary people into extraordinary lovers of God and of others." We like to say that we are here to turn people into great lovers! Our goal is for every ministry, program, and activity of the church to become a means by which people are being transformed into faithful disciples of Jesus Christ through whose lives the love of God is becoming a tangible reality in our world.

John Wesley called the process by which the Holy Spirit transforms our lives into the likeness of Christ "Christian perfection," or "being made perfect [i.e., complete, whole, mature] in love." He preached that the core of religion is "the life of God in the soul; Christ formed in the heart" ("Awake, Thou That Sleepest," *The Works of John Wesley*, volume 5, p. 30). "Such a love is this," he said, "as engrosses the whole heart, as takes up all the affections, as fills the entire capacity of the soul, and employs the utmost extent of all its faculties" ("The Almost Christian," *Works*, volume 5, p. 21).

We went back to the mission statement to describe the key elements in the heart transformation process in our congregation. Then we began asking specific questions to see how effectively each program, ministry, or activity of the church was accomplishing that task. First, let me share with you some of our reflections on the basic elements in the transformation process. Then, I will offer some "Ministry Questions" that may help you define more clearly the process by which God is at work through the mission of your church.

> *"Hyde Park United Methodist Church is a*
> *community of people . . . "*

We believe that transformation happens in community with other Christian disciples. Therefore, a central component of the process is for people to build loving, Christlike relationships with other people. Our goal is to develop Christian community in small groups. We are moving in the direction of becoming a church *of* small groups, which become the primary settings in which people experience Christian community and are sent out in ministry, rather than a church *with* small groups as one component of its life.

Ministry Question: In what specific ways does this ministry/program/activity build Christian community? What steps are being taken to develop personal, loving, caring relationships through this particular ministry?

". . . committed to Jesus Christ . . ."

Wesley said, "Faith in Christ is not barely a speculative, rational thing, a cold, lifeless assent, a train of ideas in the head; but also a disposition of the heart" ("Salvation by Faith," *Works*, volume 5, p. 9). We believe that transformation of the heart begins with a personal commitment to become a disciple of Jesus Christ. This commitment may happen in an infinite variety of ways. Our primary concern is not "how" it happens, but "that" it happens in the lives of all of our people and that people are continually challenged to move deeper into that life of discipleship.

Ministry Question: In what specific ways does this ministry/program/activity help people move toward deeper commitment to Christ, either as a beginning of the life of discipleship, or as a growing commitment of some new area in their lives?

". . . empowered by the Holy Spirit . . ."

The transformation of our lives into the likeness of Christ is not something we do, but something the Spirit of God does within us. Our task is to offer spiritual disciplines, the means of grace, and opportunities for ministry that can become settings in which the Spirit is given the freedom and opportunity to do this work in and through our lives.

Ministry Question: What are the specific ways in which this ministry/program/activity enables people to become responsive to the Spirit at work within them? How can these become means of grace in their lives? How is this ministry a witness to the meaning of our baptism? How is the grace of God that we receive in Holy Communion present in this ministry?

". . . united in the love of God . . ."

Wesley asked, "Though we cannot think alike, may we not love alike? May we not be of one heart, though we are not of one opinion? Without all doubt, we may" ("The Catholic Spirit," *Works,* volume 5, 493). The profound work of transformation that God was doing in the heart of our congregation involved learning to allow space for different convictions while being centered in the love of God in Christ. We had learned that being transformed into the likeness of Christ is not a process of making everyone agree on all of the same information, but a process by which the love of God in Christ unites different people in a common experience of grace and a common sense of mission and purpose in sharing the love of God with others.

Ministry Question: In what specific ways does this ministry/program/activity model the love of God as it accomplishes its work? Does it allow space for differences of opinion? How effectively does this ministry unite people in the common mission while allowing for the "open-minded" spirit that is a key element of our vision?

". . . called to make that love real to others . . ."

The ministries, programs, and activities of the church do not exist for their own sake, but for the larger purpose of making the love of God in Christ a tangible reality in our world. We are always "mission-directed" in meeting human need, in drawing uncommitted people into a living relationship with Christ, and in equipping committed Christians for active ministry in the world. Wesley's words from the eighteenth century provide an amazingly accurate description of the way we are called to fulfill our mission in the twenty-first century.

> Let us take a view of Christianity as spreading from one to another, and so gradually making its way into the world. . . . Supposing that these lovers of [humankind] do see "the whole

world lying in wickedness," can we believe that they would be unconcerned at the sight, at the misery of those for whom their Lord died? Would not their bowels yearn over them, and their hearts melt away for very trouble? Could they then stand idle all the day long, even were there no command from Him whom they loved? Rather would they not labour, by all possible means, to pluck some of these brands out of the burning? Undoubtedly they would: They would spare no pains to bring back whomsoever they could. . . . Those who had believed, they provoked to love and to good works; to patient continuance in well-doing. ("Scriptural Christianity," *Works*, volume 5, p. 42)

Ministry Question: How does this ministry/program/activity fulfill the mission of the church? In what specific ways does it enable us to touch other persons with the love of Christ? To what degree are decisions about this activity made in light of the perceived needs of people outside its own circle? How are people being equipped and energized for active ministries of service in the community or around the world?

> *What tangible difference do you believe your church's mission can or should make in the lives of people within it and people in the world around it?*
>
> *Have you defined the process by which God is at work in your congregation to fulfill God's vision for your congregation?*
>
> *How fully are the ministries, activities, and programs of your congregation aligned with the central mission of the church?*

It would be a great mistake, probably a sin, to give the impression that we always got it right in this process, that we have already brought all of our ministries into alignment with our mission, or that we have completely lived up to the vision that God has given us. That's simply not the case. We live in the continuing tension between what we currently are and what we believe

God would have us become. But in continuing to ask these kinds of questions, God keeps calling us back to the heart of our mission.

In the first months of the new millennium, I was preaching a series of sermons on the Revelation to John. I had spent one particular week preparing to preach on the word of the Risen Christ to the church in Ephesus: "I know your works, your toil and your patient endurance. . . . But I have this against you, that you have abandoned the love you had at first. Remember then from what you have fallen; repent, and do the works you did at first" (Revelation 2:2-5). The sermon would have to do with keeping first things first—a reminder that the main thing is to keep the main thing the main thing.

I went to bed that Saturday night with the sermon ready (or so I thought!) and with those words from the Revelation in my brain. At 1:00 A.M. I woke up in a cold sweat. (I can assure you that this doesn't happen to me very often!) I didn't actually hear a voice, but I woke up as if I had. I remembered John saying, "I was in the spirit on the Lord's day, and I heard behind me a loud voice like a trumpet" (Revelation 1:10). I can genuinely say that I felt as if God was speaking to me. I went to the computer and started typing. Here's what I heard the Spirit saying.

"You are good folks. You are doing lots of good things. You're hanging in there. You have turned from evil and are saying yes to what is good. You haven't grown weary . . . yet. But you will, if you keep going the direction you are going. You'll never be able to accomplish the mission, you'll never be able to fulfill the opportunity and to meet the needs of the people I'm sending your way if you keep going the direction you're going. It's not that you have abandoned your love for me, but that you have missed the first priority that I gave you at least five years ago when I gave you the vision, the pattern, the form I wanted you to use to fulfill this mission. Along the way, you've tinkered with it, talked about it, but have never really done it.

"Because you haven't done what I told you to do, lots of other very good things have popped up. Good things, things that respond to people's needs. People will find a way to get their needs met. But over the long haul, they are not going to be able to carry the freight, to meet the needs of all the people I want to bring to Christ through Hyde Park. They won't be effective enough as a delivery system.

"Now," the Spirit was getting a little stronger here, "it's time to stop, to remember, and to obey the vision I first gave you. It's simple. It's clear. It's time-tested. It's right out of the Methodist tradition. In fact, because the Methodists haven't been doing it, everyone else is! It will fulfill the mission and purpose of this church. It will meet people's needs. It's the vision for small communities of Christians who are making God's love real through worship, education, caring, and ministries of witness and service." It was, in fact, a vision of "Wesley Groups" that would follow the pattern of the "class meetings" or "societies" in early Methodism. So that I wouldn't miss the point, the Spirit gave specific instructions in that late night teaching session. "Here it is," he said, "for the umpteenth time.

1. Each Wesley group will connect 8 to 15 people.
2. Each Wesley group will have a facilitator/leader who will pastor that group and be accountable to one of the pastors and the gathering of leaders for support, training, encouragement, and prayer.
3. Each Wesley group will follow the pattern of the mission statement by practicing worship (they will pray), education (they will read/study/learn the Bible), caring (they will "pastor" each other), and witness/service (they will find some way of reaching out to others in the love of Christ).
4. Each Wesley group will keep an open door. They will either be open to welcoming new persons into their group or will pray for God to call someone from their group to become a leader for a new group.
5. Each Wesley group will meet at least monthly, but preferably weekly or biweekly.
6. Each Wesley group will use study resources that are consistent with our mission and our spiritual tradition.

7. Existing groups will be asked to pray for guidance as to whether they should continue as they are or reshape themselves into the Wesley group pattern. Trust them, they will figure out what to do."

Then I heard the Spirit saying, "Do it now. Between now and Ash Wednesday, I want you to:

1. Invite people to hear God's call to become leaders and to recruit their groups.
2. Invite the congregation to respond to the invitation to be in a small group for Lent.
3. Train those leaders and dedicate them on Ash Wednesday.
4. Begin with groups that meet for Lent, either as existing groups or new ones."

I thought I felt some impatience in the Spirit's voice when the message concluded, "There it is, Jim. I've given it to you before. Over the long haul, this is the first priority for this congregation fulfilling its mission. Now,

1. Call leaders.
2. Train leaders.
3. Invite people to participate.
4. Just do it!"

Like John's letter to Ephesus, this word from the Lord came with a warning and a promise. The warning is in verse 5: "If you don't do it, your lamp will go out." The promise is in verse 7: "If you do it, you will find life growing out of a tree in the garden of paradise" (author's paraphrase).

It was one of a very few times in my ministry that I laid aside most of the prepared sermon and shared the fresh word of the Spirit with the congregation. The response clearly confirmed that it was the word we needed to hear. Nearly three years later, people still talk about being obedient to the vision I received that night. We haven't yet fulfilled all of its potential, but it continues to be the goal toward which we are working.

The truth is that there's nothing all that unique about our Wesley group model. Every major movement of spiritual awakening in the his-

> *Have you had any late night visions recently? How has the Spirit spoken to you about your faithfulness to God's vision for your church?*
>
> *Is there something God has been calling you to do but you have been slow in doing?*
>
> *How effectively is your congregation developing Christian community in small groups?*

tory of the church, from Pentecost to the present, has included some expression of Christian community in small, committed, caring groups of disciples. Across the world today, wherever the church is alive and growing in ministry, the church is living out its life in some form of small group experience.

We have found that the most important and most challenging step in the process is calling and equipping leaders. As we have moved through this process, we have established the following expectations for small group leaders. You'll notice again that they follow our mission.

Expectations for Wesley Group Leaders

Every Wesley group leader is expected to be personally and passionately committed to Jesus Christ and to the mission of Hyde Park United Methodist Church through:

Worship: We are praying leaders.

Wesley group leaders are expected to:

• be faithful in corporate worship in the congregation

- develop a daily pattern of personal devotion and prayer
- pray regularly for each member of the group
- be focused in developing the spiritual life of each person in their group.

Education: We are learning leaders.

Leaders are expected to:

- read and study their Bible each day
- attend the Gathering of Adult Leaders for training and accountability
- lead their group using resources that are consistent with the mission and spiritual tradition of our congregation
- commit themselves to study and preparation for the group meetings.

(DISCIPLE Bible study is the core resource in our congregation for spiritual leaders.)

Caring: We are caring leaders.

Leaders are expected to:

- provide pastoral care to each member of the group
- equip the group to care for each other in times of need
- share with the ministry staff the word of specific need in their group.

Ministries of Witness and Service: We are called witnesses for Christ.

Leaders are expected to:

- model Christian stewardship of life by practicing disciplines that maintain personal health and wholeness

- practice or move in the direction of the biblical model of tithing as a personal spiritual discipline
- lead their group in finding practical ways to give themselves away to others in ministry through the church or in the community.

Following the same form, we defined what we believe are the minimum expectations for people who become a part of a Wesley group.

Expectations for Wesley Group Members

Members of Wesley groups will be expected to commit themselves in covenant with the other members of their group to fulfill the mission of the church through:

Worship: We will become praying people.

Group members will:

- be committed to personal and spiritual growth as a disciple of Jesus Christ
- pray daily for each member of their group
- be faithful in corporate worship in the congregation.

Education: We will become learning disciples.

Group members will:

- read their Bible each day
- give priority to their group meeting time
- study the material for their group meeting.

Caring: We will care for one another.

Group members will:

- respect the confidentiality of the group setting by never repeating anything that is said outside the meeting
- honor other group members by being on time and prepared for each group meeting
- be available to help and support other group members in times of need
- love other group members enough to respect their differences.

Witness and Service: We will be in ministry together.

Group members will:

- find practical opportunities to give themselves away to others through the ministry of the church or in the community
- maintain an open door by welcoming new persons into the group or by listening for God to call them to become the leader of another group
- develop personal disciplines that model Christian stewardship of life.

We've tried several different formats to provide support, training, and accountability for group leaders, most of which have been less than successful. However, Christ Church United Methodist, Fort Lauderdale, became the model for us (see Dick Wills, *Waking to God's Dream*, 35-47). Our most recent attempt was a monthly event that we called "GOAL: Gathering of Adult Leaders." Each gathering includes time for (you've probably come to expect this by now!) *worship,* in which we celebrate what God is doing in their groups and pray for each other, *education,* in which we offer practical training to improve the leaders' effectiveness, *caring,* in which we share specific concerns coming out of the leaders' experiences, and *witness and service,* in which we focus on how their small groups can be reaching out to the world.

As we've been moving in the direction of becoming a church *of* small groups rather than *with* small groups, we've expanded this monthly gathering to include Wesley group leaders, Sunday school teachers, DISCIPLE Bible study facilitators, and ministry team leaders so that all of the leadership of the church is connected in this gathering.

Here's the truth: We aren't there yet! We're still working on it. At the time of this writing, our Committee on Lay Leadership is involved in concentrated study and reflection on how best to call, equip, train, and support servant leaders in ministry through the congregation. Our hope is that we will develop practical processes by which we raise the quality of leadership in every area of ministry. We're not yet sure what form it will take, but we know that this is the vision and we continue to move in that direction. Perhaps sharing some of the most common questions and concerns we face will be a way for you to use our experience in your own setting.

WHY ARE WE SO INTENT ON DEVELOPING COMMUNITY IN SMALL GROUPS?

Theologically, our need for community is rooted in our understanding of the nature of the Triune God. L. Gregory Jones writes, "at the heart of the Christian doctrine of God is the conviction that God lives as the loving friendships, the self-giving relationships, of Father, Son and Holy Spirit . . . God is God as the endless and ever new self-giving among Father, Son and Spirit" (*Embodying Forgiveness*, pp. 112-13). Throughout the Bible, living in covenant with God always involves living in covenant with others. Practically, the evidence of church history is that living in community with other disciples is the most effective way to transform ordinary people into extraordinary lovers of God and of others. In small groups, people experience the love of God, are formed as Christian disciples, and are equipped for ministry in the world.

IS THE GROUP SELECTION PROCESS OPEN WITH GROUPS ADVERTISED OR IS THERE A POINT PERSON WHO ASSIGNS PEOPLE TO GROUPS?

We find every possible way of communicating the need for every growing disciple to be in a small group and encourage every person to participate, but we generally do not publicize the specific groups. The pastors, director of adult education, and lay coordinators help people find the most appropriate group for them.

WHAT IS THE FORMAT AND LENGTH OF MEETINGS?

It varies, but the normal pattern would be to meet weekly or twice a month for approximately 90 minutes. Each group designs its own format, but every group meeting would include prayer (worship), Bible study (education), time for personal sharing of growth and concerns (caring), and some focus on reaching out in ministry (witness and service).

HOW DO WE MAINTAIN ACCOUNTABILITY?

Trust and accountability are crucial. The leaders are accountable to the pastors and other small group leaders in the monthly gathering for spiritual support, nurture, and training. Group members are accountable to each other for their confidentiality and support.

WHAT ABOUT CURRICULUM? ARE STUDIES ASSIGNED OR DO GROUPS CHOOSE THEIR OWN?

Our approach is to outline some basic resources to get the groups started, after which each group chooses resources from those that are available from the director of adult education. The pastors are ultimately responsible for determining whether resources are consistent with our identity and mission.

HOW ARE LEADERS SELECTED OR SCREENED?

Leaders are recommended by members of small groups, recruited by the small group leaders, or recognized in the gift discernment process. Ultimately, the pastors and director of adult education give their approval of group leaders. All of our leaders go through liability screening.

WHAT ABOUT A PROTOTYPE GROUP COMPOSED OF POTENTIAL LEADERS IN
WHICH THEY CAN EXPERIENCE WHAT IT WILL BE LIKE?

Definitely. In one sense, every small group is a prototype for
leaders. Every person who leads a group should have already
experienced one. But we also create small groups of people who
were specifically chosen as potential leaders. The experience in
that small group clarified their calling to be a leader. Two of the
leaders who met in one of those groups later became husband and
wife!

DO GROUPS HAVE A LIFECYCLE? ARE THEY ALLOWED TO DIE?

Yes. When a group has fulfilled its mission, we encourage people to either move to other groups or to consider disbanding so
that each person in that group can become a leader of a new one.
As some groups die, others grow. Only the kingdom of God lasts
forever! If the horse is dead, dismount.

HOW ABOUT ADDING NEW MEMBERS TO EXISTING GROUPS?

Yes and no. It's up to the group. While we always want the
group to have an open door, that doesn't necessarily mean that
every group is in a place to integrate a new person into their experience. Sometimes it means sending one of their group members
out to start a new group.

WHAT ABOUT SHORT-TERM AND SPECIAL INTEREST GROUPS?

Wesley groups are intended to be long-term, ongoing communities for growing disciples. We also see a need for short-term
and special interest groups that often become the entry point into
the ongoing csommunity life of our congregation. These include
"Fresh Start," an eight-week series designed to introduce the
basic affirmations of the faith to searching people; "New Member
Orientation," a six-week series that is required of all persons
before becoming members of our congregation; *Network* (Willow

Creek Resources), the process by which we help people discover their place in ministry; and *Companions in Christ* (Upper Room Ministries), a focused experience in spiritual formation. Special interest groups include Christian Peacemakers, Mid-Single Connection, MOM's Group, men's groups, groups for parents of children and youth, and Senior Adult Fellowship. Our goal, however, is that every group will live out of the vision for worship, education, caring, and service.

Like the mission statement itself, we know that the vision for transformation in small groups is taking hold when we hear it coming back from the congregation. Three years after my "Saturday night live" experience with the Spirit, talking about small groups is becoming a basic element in our congregational culture. We look forward to the day when one of the most common questions in our congregation will be, "Tell me about your small group." Most important, we are seeing hearts transformed by the love of God in the process.

- How would you know if you were accomplishing your mission? Do you have a defined process by which your mission is being fulfilled?
- How would you know if you had succeeded in your mission? What difference would you see in people and in the community you serve?
- How is the community life of your congregation? Are people experiencing spiritual growth and being sent out in ministry through small groups?

CHAPTER 10

Doing a New Thing

Most of us are about as eager to be changed as we were to be born,
and go through our changes in a similar state of shock.

—James Baldwin, *Context*

The truth about some of us most of the time and most of us at least some of the time is that we're not all that wild about change, particularly when change involves something with which we are familiar, something comfortable, something we have known, respected, trusted, or loved over time.

In 1912, the nations of Europe were preparing for what would become the most horrendous war the world had ever seen. In France, one of the major debates related to the color of military uniforms. The British had finally traded in their red coats for khaki. The Germans were changing from bright Prussian blue to field-gray. Both colors would eventually become nearly invisible in the mud of the trenches. Meanwhile, the French were still wearing the same bright red caps and red trousers they had worn for generations.

When the French Minister of War recommended that they change to gray-blue or gray-green, the nation rose up in protest. A parliamentary hearing was called in which a retired military leader declared, "Eliminate the red trousers? Never! *Le pantalon rouge c'est la France!*" One newspaper declared that trading "all that is colorful, all that gives the soldier his vivid aspect" for some muddy, inglorious color, was "contrary both to French taste and military function." The Minister of War tried to point out that in this case "French taste" and "military function" might not be the same thing, but the opposition was immovable. The French army went to war with their red trousers. Later, the Minister of War wrote, "That blind . . . attachment to the most visible of all colors was to have cruel consequences." Given the slaughter of French solders on the Western front, his words still sound like an understatement of gruesome reality (Barbara W. Tuchman, *The Guns of August*, pp. 37-38).

What are the "red trousers" in your congregation? What might be the consequences of your loyalty to them?

Where do you experience the tension between tradition and change, taste and function, mission and method; between something old and something new?

It was, to be sure, a small detail, but in the history of the events leading up to World War I, the French loyalty to their red trousers stands out as an historic example of the tension between tradition and change, taste and function, mission and method; between something old and something new.

It's encouraging to know that Jesus faced the same kind of tension. He stood firmly within the old way of Hebrew tradition. In the Sermon on the Mount, he said that he did not come to destroy the law, but to fulfill it. But in the act of fulfilling the covenant, Jesus kept running against the grain of more than 600 rules of practice and behavior that had accumulated around the central core of the tradition. The coming of God's reign in Jesus meant changing the rules of practice that had become so familiar to the Jewish people. Matthew invites us into two scenes in Jesus' life that portray that tension. They may speak to the kind of transformation that needs to happen in your congregation.

The first scene is a dinner party at Matthew's house. The former tax collector was so excited about his new life as a disciple that he invited all his friends to meet Jesus. The problem was that because Matthew was a tax collector, most of his friends were tax collectors, too. They were the kind of people any kosher-keeping

Jew would have seen as a very motley crowd. The tradition-bound Pharisees, whose primary concern was protecting their own purity from contamination by sinful people, were utterly appalled. They asked, "Why does your teacher eat with . . . sinners?" Before the disciples could answer, Jesus answered the question. He reached back into the Old Testament tradition and reminded them that only the sick need a physician. He quoted the words of the prophet, Hosea, who told the people that God puts a higher priority on mercy than on sacrifice (Matthew 9:11-13, Hosea 6:6).

Jesus drew from the core of the old tradition to defend his new way of relating to others. He used the words of the prophet to declare the passionate mercy of God that welcomes every person who longs for the healing power of the kingdom of God. The mercy of God, proclaimed by the prophets, meant that the old boundaries had to be broken down so that everyone could be welcomed into the new life of the Kingdom.

In the second scene, the followers of John the Baptist noticed that Jesus and his disciples were not keeping the rules about fasting. My guess is that they were jealous. It was like being on a strict diet and seeing everyone else going to a banquet. They wanted to know, "Why do we . . . fast often, but your disciples do not fast?" (Matthew 9:14). Jesus reminded them that the tradition said that it was permissible to break the fast when the bridegroom came for the wedding feast. He was pointing to his own presence among the disciples. Why should his disciples fast, which bears witness to the longing for God, when the kingdom of God was present among them? The presence of the kingdom of God in human experience is cause for rejoicing and feasting.

> *How much of your congregation's tradition are you willing to change in order to welcome new people into the kingdom of God?*
>
> *Does your congregation have a passion for welcoming spiritually hungry people to the table of God's mercy the way Matthew invited that crowd to his dinner party?*

In both scenes, Jesus used the core reality of their heritage as justification for breaking the rules of practice that had accumulated around it. The new life of the Kingdom could not be contained within the old boundaries of their rules of behavior. Obedience to the core of biblical principle meant changes in biblical practice. (See Peter Gomes, *The Good Book*, chapter 4, for a more thorough discussion of the difference between principle and practice.)

John Wesley was a prim, proper little Anglican priest who was convinced that the gospel could only be preached in a consecrated pulpit in the Church of England. But then George Whitefield invited him to come out to the fields where he was preaching to poor people and coal miners. When Wesley saw the way these common people experienced the love of God in Christ he wrote that he "consented to become more vile" in order to share the love of God with everyone. It was right in the spirit of what Jesus did at Matthew's dinner party. And it was in that spirit that Wesley told his preachers:

> You have nothing to do but to save souls. Therefore spend and be spent in this work . . . It is not your business to preach so many times, and to take care of this or that society; but to save as many souls as you can; to bring as many sinners as you possibly can to repentance, and with all your power to build them up in that holiness without which they cannot see the Lord. (Quoted in *Leadership in the Wesleyan Spirit*, p. 124)

The critical question confronting leaders in most mainline, long-established churches is how willing we are to change our methods in order to fulfill our mission—specifically, the mission of sharing the love of God in Christ with people who have not yet experienced it.

While working on this book I attended a United Methodist Annual Conference in the Southeast. Better known as the "Bible belt," the Southeastern and Southcentral jurisdictions are the only areas of the nation in which Methodism is showing significant growth. But at this conference, it was announced that over four hundred churches had not received a single person into the church by confession of faith. Four hundred churches had not found a way to confirm a young person in the faith or to welcome a new disciple of Jesus Christ. A young pastor who was being ordained into the ministry that day said, "Mr. Wesley must be rolling over in his grave!"

My concern is not about numerical growth for the institutional church. My concern is for mainline congregations that have apparently lost a passion for sharing the love of God in Christ with spiritually searching people in their communities and about finding ways to engage those persons in a process of discipleship that will equip them to become the agents of God's love in the world. My guess is that many of those four hundred churches were taking care of a lot of good things. I would bet that the preacher's salaries were paid, the carpets were cleaned, and the buildings were maintained. My guess is that some of them have pretty good choirs that sing pretty good music, and pretty good preachers who preach pretty good sermons. But they have lost their focus on the core mission Jesus gave to the church when he said, "Go therefore and make disciples" (Matthew 28:19).

The tragedy of this lack of passion is exacerbated by the reality of the spiritual hunger of the culture around us. We are a spiritually saturated culture where spiritually hungry people are being forced to survive on "junk food" for the soul. (See chapter 7 in my book, *Passion, Power, and Praise* for a discussion of spiritual "junk food.")

In my first meeting with the leadership of Hyde Park Church, I asked why they had requested the bishop to appoint me as their pastor. The answer was that during the thirteen years I had served in Orlando, St. Luke's Church had seen significant growth, and they wanted their congregation to grow. I thought for a moment and then had one of those moments of inspiration that never seem to come often enough. I replied, "Just about every church I know *says* they want to grow, but that's not the real question. The real question is whether we are willing to make the kind of changes that might make growth possible. My guess is that it will take us at least a year to discover the answer to that question." As time would confirm, this would become the defining question for us in the tension between tradition and change, mission and method, principle and practice.

Jesus spoke directly to that kind of tension by drawing on a very common, everyday experience. He said it's just like trying to sew a new, unshrunken patch onto an old, well-worn garment. The first time you throw it in the laundry, the patch will shrink and tear the whole coat apart. It's like putting new, unfermented wine into stiff, old wineskins. As the new wine ferments, it expands. When it expands, it will tear apart the inflexible wineskins and you will end up losing both. "New wine," he said, "is put into fresh wineskins, and so both are preserved" (Matthew 9:17).

Did you notice the way Jesus said that "both are preserved"? He valued both the old wineskins and the new power of the fermenting wine. He affirmed the long tradition in which he stood, but also affirmed the way the new life of the Kingdom forms new practices. In both his practice and his words, Jesus held in tension the long tradition out of which he had come and the new life he came to bring. He claimed both the core of the covenant that had been handed down to him and revealed the new ways in which that covenant would be lived in the world. He held together tradition and change, mission and method, the old and the new.

James Collins and Jerry Porras spent six years studying some of the finest corporations in America to discover why some corporations continue to thrive over time while others that had an equally good beginning passed away. They said that the single most important discovery they made was that the thriving corporations have a clearly defined, core ideology of mission and identity. That central core of who they are and why they are here is irrevocable and unchanging. At the same time, they are willing to change just about everything they do in order to accomplish that mission. Product lines, organizational structure, marketing processes—everything is up for change to enable them to effectively fulfill their core mission. They condensed their discovery in the phrase, "Preserve the Core/Stimulate Progress" (*Built to Last*, p. 89).

They also found that the companies that get into trouble are the ones that confuse their core mission with specific practices, the way the French military confused French taste with military function. "A visionary company carefully preserves and protects its core ideology, yet all the specific *manifestations* (italic theirs) of its core ideology must be open for change and evolution" (p. 81).

It's fair to say that many churches, if not most, have a hard time on this one. We get so accustomed to specific practices that we start to think we cannot be effective without them. Take adult Sunday school classes, for instance. Hyde Park Church was blessed to have a strong tradition of adult Sunday school classes in which people were growing in their faith and experiencing genuine Christian community.

But then we started offering DISCIPLE Bible study, an intensive, thirty-four-week process of biblical study that requires people to make a commitment to spend time in daily reflection on Scripture and to attend a two-and-a-half hour group gathering each week. Most of the people in DISCIPLE had not been active in a Sunday school class, but some were. Some of them dropped out of Sunday school to be in DISCIPLE. Then we added the contemporary worship service during the traditional Sunday school hour, and some of the people who usually went to Sunday school chose to go to that service.

Suddenly, some of the adult class leaders felt threatened and were upset that we were not protecting adult Sunday school. So, we went back to the mission, which said that we are "Making God's Love Real" through "educational opportunities that enable people to grow as faithful disciples and equip them for ministry in the world." Some people thought the mission was to get people in to Sunday school. But Sunday school is a method, not the mission. Sunday school has been, and for many folks will continue to be, a very effective means by which we accomplish our mission. But if I had to choose between people spending two-and-a-half hours each week in a DISCIPLE group or one hour of study (well, it's more like 30-40 minutes when you take out time for coffee and late-comers!) in Sunday school, I would go with DISCIPLE every time. But my first preference is to provide multiple methods to accomplish a single mission. If the method works, we keep it. If it doesn't work, we let it go.

The good news for us is that over time, our adult Sunday school classes have also continued to grow as we have added more options at alternative hours. We simply couldn't find anything in Scripture or our tradition that said that 9:30 Sunday school was the *only* method for accomplishing the mission.

Bill Easum describes the same reality with a different analogy in his book *Sacred Cows Make Gourmet Burgers*. "Ministries and styles of leadership that once appeared to work well no longer produce the desired results. . . . Simply learning to do old chores faster or to be able to adapt old forms to more complex situations no longer produces the desired results" (p. 21).

> *What will "Preserve the Core/Stimulate Progress" look like in your congregation?*

"Preserve the Core/Stimulate Progress" sounds to me like a corporate illustration of the principle behind these parables about the tension between the old and the new. Jesus calls us to preserve the core of God's covenant with us. That covenant is irrevocable and unchanging. At the same time, he challenges us to be open to new ways to share that core reality of God's love with an ever changing but always hungry world. By holding those two realities together, we preserve both the wine and the wineskins. Through that creative tension the Spirit of God can be at work among us.

Most biblical scholars agree that Matthew's Gospel is not just recording an event in the life of Jesus. They assume that this Gospel also reflects the tension that existed within the life of the early church around the time that this Gospel was written. The followers of Jesus were wrestling with what it would mean to be faithful to the core of the tradition they had received from the past and at the same time live fully and freely in the new life of the Kingdom revealed in Jesus. The tension in the story reflected the tension within the church. If Matthew's Gospel reflects the tension in the early church, there's a good chance that it reflects the

Doing a New Thing

ongoing tension in the church in every age, which means that it speaks to us, too.

It's pretty obvious that Hyde Park Church values tradition. We minister in an historically designated building in the historical district of one of the oldest cities in Florida. We have a pretty clear sense of who we have been. Through the process described previously, we now have clarity about who we are and why we are here. Those things are unchanging. We will, at all costs, preserve that core. But as we have received more clarity about who God is calling us to be, we've been going through some of the most radical changes in our history. We've made changes in our organization and decision-making structure, changes in our worship styles, changes in learning opportunities, changes in the way we care for each other, changes in publicity and advertising, and changes in the way we welcome new people and engage them in the process of discipleship.

We spent eighteen months answering the questions, *Who are we?* and *Why are we here?* Then we began asking, *What are we to do? What kind of ministries and programs would best accomplish that mission?* We spent another year evaluating what we were doing and how other folks were doing similar ministry, and outlining the steps we would need to take to begin fulfilling that mission. For what it's worth, here's the way we answered that question.

Fulfilling the Mission: Making God's Love Real

Worship

We will continue to worship in the liturgical tradition of the Methodist-Anglican branch of the Protestant Reformation. At the same time, we will be open to new, creative, and exciting alternatives in music and worship that will relate to the changing population around us while maintaining our focus on our mission of glorifying God, celebrating the faith, and inviting others to faith in Christ. Because we believe that worship is the "act of the people," we will find creative ways for people to use their gifts and talents in worship.

WHAT IT WILL TAKE
- Multiple worship services, providing alternatives for time and style of worship
- Expansion of the music ministry to include a wide variety of opportunities for people to use their gifts in the ministry of worship
- Expansion of program/ministry staff in worship
- Major renovation of the sanctuary to provide for physical accessibility; flexibility; adequate "people flow" to enhance Christian community; adequate space for choirs, instruments, and other musical events; and audio-video capability

Education

We will provide a strong program of Christian education for all ages and for a wide variety of people. It will be based on disciplined study of the Bible along with opportunities for study in Christian theology, church history, Christian social and ethical concerns, and practical areas such as parenting and family concerns.

DISCIPLE Bible study will be the core resource for personal spiritual growth, and it will be the basis upon which people discover their calling to live out their discipleship in ministry.

CHILDREN'S MINISTRIES WILL INCLUDE:
- multiple sessions in relationship to the worship services
- expansion of Small Blessings Preschool
- development of weekday education experiences for younger children
- summer programs for children from the neighborhoods around us

YOUTH MINISTRIES WILL INCLUDE:
- development of a broadly based youth ministry so that the church becomes the central focus of the lives of our youth
- Bible study, fellowship groups, recreational programs, mission/ministry opportunities, music/drama/arts programs

ADULT MINISTRIES WILL INCLUDE:
- opportunities for Christian growth at each level of adult experience
- special focus on college/early career young adults
- singles' ministries
- continuing education for older adults
- opportunities for seminary-level studies for mature adults

WHAT IT WILL TAKE
- Major expansion of program staff
- Construction of a new building for preschool, children, and youth activities; recreation and fellowship; creative use of media in education; and accessibility for children and older adults. (Note: A ministry of this scope cannot be accomplished within the constraints of the present facilities.)

Caring Ministries

We will express the Spirit of Christ in caring and compassionate ministries within and through our congregation.
- Stephen Ministry will be a primary means by which we provide care to persons in crisis and be a model for persons to be trained to use their gifts in caring ministries
- We will find active ways to care for persons through groups such as AA, Al Anon, and Overcomers
- We will create ministries for specific groups such as

parents of children with special needs, widows/widowers, and families of drug abusers

WHAT IT WILL TAKE
- Development of spiritual support ministries of prayer and spiritual discipline
- Development of small groups
- Commitment to lay caring on the part of the entire congregation
- Expansion of lay involvement in ministry
- Staff support for caring ministries

Witness and Service

We will "make disciples" by drawing uncommitted persons to Jesus Christ and by being in ministry to the needs of our city and our world.

EVANGELISM:
- Outreach to the growing young adult singles population in our area
- Creative use of radio and television in our metropolitan area
- Overall advertising plan to let people know we are here
- Focus on music and the arts

COMMUNITY MINISTRIES:
- Involvement of church members in active ministries related to the needs of our city including homeless concerns, education, racial concerns, and the environment
- Cooperation with other churches and community service agencies to meet human need

GLOBAL MINISTRIES:
- Continued support of the global ministries of the United Methodist Church
- Support and involvement in specific mission projects selected by the local church

- Involvement of our people as Volunteers in Mission
- Emphasis on youth hearing God's call to mission and ministry

WHAT IT WILL TAKE
- Support for creative uses of media
- Technical equipment for media ministries
- Ministry staff expansion
- High level volunteer participation
- Courageous commitment to interracial ministries

Eight years have passed since we prepared these goals. A few of them have been modified along the way, but for the most part, they continue to be the framework for our ministry. Looking back across them, several lessons stand out for me to pass on to you.

1. LIVING THE MISSION MEANS TALKING THE MISSION.

Notice the way everything in this document grows out of and reinforces the mission of "Making God's Love Real" through ministries of worship, education, caring, and witness and service. We were absolutely determined to live the mission of the church and to align everything we did with it. One of the ways to do that is to consistently talk the language of the mission. People will be more likely to accept change if they can see it as a direct fulfillment of their mission. We knew that the mission was taking hold when we started hearing it coming back from the congregation.

2. REMEMBER THAT THE BEST SURPRISE IS NO SURPRISE.

Unless it's their birthday, most people don't really like being surprised. These proposals emerged as we studied our ministries in light of our mission. The "What Will It Take" sections were general enough to allow changes to develop in their own time, but they were specific enough to let people see the changes that would be coming. Long before the changes actually came, this material laid the groundwork for them. No one was surprised when we started planning alternative worship services or building renovations. They had known it was coming all the time. More important, there was no question that we moved from mission to ministry and then to the specific changes that would make that ministry happen.

3. CREATE OPPORTUNITIES FOR BUY-IN.

Even now, reading back across these lines, I can remember some of the discussion in staff meetings, committees, and small groups. Like the drafts of the mission statement, this material was printed in the newsletter and shared with small groups so that everyone had the opportunity for feedback along the way. That doesn't mean that everyone got what they wanted, but it did mean that everyone had the opportunity to be heard. Allowing time for people to think, talk, and engage in the process meant that no one had to "sell" the proposals to resistant customers. Rather, they defined on paper what had been emerging by consensus along the way.

4. WATCH FOR "CRITICAL MASS."

I wish I could remember who told me that you don't really need a unanimous vote, though it's nice when you can get one! In fact, you don't need a majority of the people to be on board with you through the process. All you need is "critical mass." Critical mass happens when a vision begins to take hold in the heart of the congregation. It's not so much about numbers as it is about spirit. When critical mass occurs, the movement begins. There will still be people who are opposed, but critical mass will find a way to make it happen. Your job as a spiritual leader is to watch for critical mass and let it happen!

5. STICK WITH JESUS.

Bill Easum and Tom Bandy are two of the leading spokespersons for change in the church in America today. They consistently insist that "change must be anchored in the experience of the congregation with Jesus." They are convinced that the key question for congregational transformation goes to the heart of its Christology: "What is it about our experience with Jesus that this community cannot live without?" Bandy declares, "No enduring change can happen in the church, no matter how large or small, without it being linked to continuing spiritual growth in one's relationship with Jesus" (*Moving Off the Map*, pp. 21-22).

- Have you begun to define your ministries on the basis of your mission? Is the language of your mission beginning to permeate the linguistic culture of your congregation?
- Have you developed an eye for "critical mass" and for the movement of the Spirit in your congregation?
- To what degree would you identify with these words of John Henry, Cardinal Newman? "We do not like to be new-made; we are afraid of it; it is throwing us out of all our natural ways, of all that is familiar to us. . . . In a higher world it is otherwise, but here below to live is to change, and to be perfect is to have changed often" ("Is Your Clay Moist?").

CHAPTER 11

Worship That Goes to the Heart

Worship is the submission of all our nature to God. It is the quicken-
ing of conscience by his holiness; the nourishment of mind with his
truth; the purifying of the imagination by his beauty; the opening of
the heart to his love; the surrender of will to his purpose—and all of
this gathered up in adoration, the most selfless emotion of which our
nature is capable and therefore the chief remedy of that self-centered-
ness which is our original sin.
—Archbishop William Temple, *The Oxford Book of Prayer*

The truth about every one of us is that we have an innate and inescapable need to worship. We are created that way. Saint Augustine said, "Lord, you have put salt on our tongues so that we will be thirsty for you." The hunger for a living relationship with God is imbedded in the genetic code of the human family. We *will* give worth, ultimate value, and personal commitment to something or someone. The question is not *whether* we will worship, but *what, whom,* and *how* we will worship. The defining theological issue of our time is not atheism but idolatry.

On the Sunday following September 11, 2001, every preacher with a pulpit attempted to place the horror of that day in some kind of theological perspective. With painful honesty, Randy Ashcraft, a Baptist pastor in my neighborhood, identified the World Trade Center and the Pentagon as "the twin towers of our cultural idolatry." I reminded our congregation of the two places where the Gospel writers record that Jesus wept.

The first time Jesus wept was when he stood beside the grave of his friend Lazarus. There Jesus shared the painful reality of our helplessness in the face of death. The second was the day of that palm-waving procession into Jerusalem when the people shouted, "Blessed is the king who comes in the name of the Lord! Peace in heaven, and glory in the highest heaven!" (Luke 19:38). But Jesus wasn't cheering. He knew that the road he was following would lead inexorably to a cross.

When Jesus came down the Mount of Olives, he saw the Holy City spread out before him in the clear light of the morning sun. The view was guaranteed to take away the breath of every patriotic, faithful Jew. It was like looking across the Hudson River to the skyline of New York City or standing on the sloping hills of Arlington Cemetery to look across the Potomac to Washington, D.C. Luke records that when Jesus saw the city, "he wept over it, saying, 'If you, even you, had only recognized on this day the things that make for peace!' " (Luke 19:42).

The first time Jesus wept his tears were pastoral. They were tears of compassion for our suffering and pain. The second time Jesus wept, his tears were prophetic. They were tears of regret over our human inclination to worship the wrong things. Bringing that story into our experience, I said:

It's clear that the people who attacked our cities on Tuesday were fanatics—so fanatical that they were willing to die for their destructive ideology. It's pretty clear that they were radical fundamentalists. Like all radical fundamentalists—whether they are Americans who abuse the name of Christianity or Muslims who abuse the name of Islam—the one thing they have in common is their absolute conviction that theirs is the only truth and that it must be defended at all costs. They were fanatics and they were radical fundamentalists, but they were not stupid.

They knew what they were doing. They hit us where they knew it would hurt the most. They hit us in the two cities that symbolize our national life and values more dramatically than any others. They hit us in the symbols of the two things in which this culture actually places its trust: our economic power and our military might. You want to hurt Americans? Attack our worship of materialism and militarism.

In the time that has passed since the towers fell, I've seen nothing to contradict and more than enough to confirm that analysis. We sing "God Bless America," we print "In God We Trust" on our money, we rise up to defend the words "under God" in the Pledge of Allegiance, but when the going gets tough, our default position is to put our ultimate trust in our economic power and our military might. Worship gets confused with patriotism; the flag takes priority over the cross.

On a more personal level, some of us worship our careers. Some of us give first priority to our wealth. Some of us give the place of highest honor to our education. Some of us place ultimate value in sexual pleasure. Some of us worship our families. Sometimes

> *What or whom do you really worship? To what or to whom do you give ultimate value?*

> *What effect did 9/11 have on your experience with God? What do you believe are the most common forms of idolatry in our culture today?*

religious folks worship at the altar of denominational loyalty. In and of themselves, these are all good things. But not one of them is worthy of our worship. Not one of them is good enough or great enough to take the place of God. And not one of them will satisfy the deepest hunger of our souls, namely, our soul-hunger for a living, loving, growing relationship with God.

Our soul-hunger for God is at the heart of the fascination with spirituality that is sweeping across the country today. Unfortunately, according to Episcopal Bishop Claude E. Payne, "the mainline denominations have not effectively responded to America's spiritual hunger, nor are they positioning themselves to do so" (*Reclaiming the Great Commission*, p. 6). A critical step in satisfying that spiritual hunger must be a renewal of worship. Congregational cardiology creates worship that goes all the way to the heart.

Throughout the church today, pastors, musicians, seminary professors, and faithful laity are debating the merits or deficiencies of "traditional," "contemporary," or "blended" styles of worship. Everywhere I go I hear pastors talking about starting a "contemporary" service, often with little or no serious consideration as to why they are doing it. I also hear people defending "traditional" worship with very little biblical reflection in their defense of it. It's clear to me that the critical issues go much deeper than whether we use the technology of the sixteenth century (the pipe organ) or the technology of the twenty-first century (video projectors and computers). What really matters goes beyond whether we sing hymns from books or praise choruses from a screen. Those are matters of method and style. What matters most is the clarity of mission upon which those methods are chosen. The heart-level questions are not *whether* our services are traditional or contemporary but *why* we do what we do and *what* we hope God will do in the lives of people through our worship.

In thinking about the kind of worship that goes to the heart, let's begin with the story of Moses' experience with God at the burning bush recorded in Exodus 3:1-15. As I live with this dramatic story in the light of our experience of congregational cardiology, four key challenges underlie our understanding of worship.

Open Your Eyes: Worship Cultivates Awareness

Notice what Moses did when he came upon the burning bush. "[Moses] looked. . . . Then Moses said, 'I must turn aside and look at this great sight, and see why the bush is not burned up'" (Exodus 3:2).

Have you ever wondered how many other shepherds might have walked past that burning bush but were too busy tending their sheep to notice that it was on fire? Have you ever asked how long that bush might have kept on burning if Moses hadn't seen it? The critical moment in the story was when Moses turned aside

from the ordinary pattern of his life to look and to see why the
bush wasn't consumed. Worship should challenge us to turn
aside from our ordinary patterns and open our eyes to see the
presence of God.

I once heard William Willimon, the prolific Dean of the
Chapel at Duke University, define worship as "learning to pay
attention." Worship—corporate worship in the congregation and
personal worship through the disciplines of prayer and meditation—is the process by which we turn aside from the distractions
of our lives and open our eyes to see what God is doing around
us. It's the discipline through which we silence the cacophony of
our contemporary existence and listen for the voice of God.
Elizabeth Barrett Browning wrote:

> Earth's crammed with heaven,
> And every common bush afire with God;
> But only he who sees takes off his shoes;
> The rest sit round it and pluck blackberries.

("Aurora Leigh")

I'm convinced that people in our day are hungry for experiences in worship that will open their eyes to see things they otherwise would never see. Moses simply looked. And did you
notice how God responded? "When the LORD saw that he had
turned aside to see, God called to him out of the bush" (3:4).

The Almighty God waited until Moses turned aside to see.
Then God spoke to him. Every
now and then someone asks me,
"Jim, why don't we hear God
speaking to us today the way he
spoke to people in the Bible?"
My answer is that it's because
we aren't paying attention.

> *How effectively does your worship enable people to perceive God's presence in the ordinary places of their lives?*

Worship cultivates our awareness of God. It challenges us to
open our eyes.

Once God got his attention, Moses was able to hear God saying, "Come no closer! Remove the sandals from your feet, for the

place on which you are standing is holy ground" (3:5). The Exodus storyteller says that "Moses hid his face, for he was afraid to look at God" (3:6). That leads us to the second challenge.

Take Off Your Shoes: Worship Ignites Awe

Genuine worship ignites within us a sense of awe, wonder, and mystery at the greatness and goodness of God. It breaks through the crust of our ordinary lives and lifts us out of ourselves so that we can know and experience God. It challenges us to take off our shoes because we know we are standing on holy ground.

In the Middle Ages, perpendicular Gothic architecture was designed to accomplish that purpose. Common people, ordinary folks who spent their days in the filth and dust of their bland, earth-toned existence would walk into a cathedral and feel themselves being lifted into a larger, higher, greater, and more beautiful world than they could have imagined. In the stained glass windows they would experience colors that they never saw anywhere else. And it still works today. Walk into any of the great cathedrals and you'll feel it. The lines draw us out of ourselves into the mystery, wonder, and beauty of the presence of God. Genuine worship has that same effect. It ignites within us the kind of awe that caused Moses to take off his shoes because he knew he was on holy ground.

But it doesn't take a cathedral. The critical shift is to remember that postmodern people are not looking for more cognitive information about God; they are searching for a heart-level experience with God. This experience of wonder and awe can happen almost anywhere, through almost any style of worship. Jason Moore says that "digital age worship needs to recapture the emotive power of the wonder and awe of God and the majesty of creation." He is convinced that this sense of awe has very little to do with debates over "traditional" versus "contemporary" worship. He describes it as "a sense of discovery that we felt the first time we saw the ocean as a child" (*Digital Storytellers*, p. 75).

Our congregation is currently worshiping in our activities center during the renovation of our sanctuary. It's an ordinary, beige-colored space with basketball backboards on either end of the room and portable dividers blocking the entrance to the kitchen. But nearly every week I talk with people who have worshiped with us for the first time who tell me that they were lifted into an experience of God that had touched their hearts. They felt the presence of God, which ignited awe within their souls.

The Methodist Awakening began when John Wesley, in an ordinary room with a group of ordinary people, felt his heart strangely warmed. Something about worship ought to warm our hearts and make us tingle in our bones. It may not happen for every person in every service. Some of us will "tingle" more than

> *When was the last time your worship experience ignited a sense of awe and wonder in your soul? How often are people lifted out of themselves and into the presence of God in your church's worship services?*

others. But one of the key elements in a biblical experience of worship is a deep sense of awe and wonder in our awareness of the greatness and goodness of God.

Having experienced the presence of God, the third challenge turns our attention to the world around us.

Listen for the Cry: Worship Energizes Compassion

The voice in the burning bush spoke out of the infinite compassion of the Almighty God. "I have observed the misery of my people who are in Egypt; I have heard their cry on account of their taskmasters. Indeed, I know their sufferings, and I have come down to deliver them" (Exodus 3:7-8).

Here's the good news. God hears our cries. God knows our suffering. And God comes in infinite love to meet us in this broken, hurting world to deliver us. Worship that is centered in the love of God in Christ will break our hearts with the things that break the heart of God. It will energize within us the same compassion that moved Jesus to grieve at Lazarus's tomb and to weep over the city of Jerusalem. The more deeply we are drawn into the passionate love of God for this whole bruised and broken creation, the more deeply we will feel the pain, the hurt, and the suffering of others.

Genuine worship is not a spiritual vacation in a "Magic Kingdom" where the people are always smiling, the streets are always clean, and every story has a happy ending. Rather, worship is the place where God meets us in the rough, messy, confused stuff of our real human existence. It is the moment in which God hears the cries of those who suffer and energizes a new level of compassion for a broken and hurting world.

I once heard the nationally known evangelist, Tony Campolo, tell about the time he was preaching in a church where no one really seemed to care. He told the congregation, "The world is going to hell and most of the people inside the church don't give a damn." He paused. Then he said, "And you know what's even worse? A whole lot of you are more concerned that I said 'damn' in church than you are that people are going to hell." He had a point. The love of God will energize a compassion within us that is like the compassion of the God who said, "I have heard their cry. I know their sufferings."

During the most difficult days of apartheid in South Africa, the congregation at Central Methodist Mission in Johannesburg placed on the altar a large, white candle surrounded with barbed wire, similar to the symbol for Amnesty International. Each Sunday, they would light the candle and call out the names of the people they knew who had been harassed, imprisoned, beaten, or murdered that week in the struggle against the powers of evil. And each week they

How does your congregation acknowledge the pain, suffering, and injustice of the world in worship?

When have you experienced worship that broke your heart with the things that break the heart of God?

would offer a prayer of hope for the day when peace and justice would come. I'll never forget standing at that altar, lighting that candle, and sensing that, in that moment of worship, all of the power of God's goodness was present with that congregation in the struggle against the power of evil. It was a reminder that God hears the cries of God's people and promises to deliver them. It was the sign of the light that shines in the darkness with the promise that the darkness will never overcome it.

If our worship energizes us with the compassion of Christ, we are then challenged to do something with that compassion, which brings us to the fourth challenge in worship.

Get Up and Go: Worship Motivates Ministry

Finally, Moses heard God say, "Come, I will send you to Pharaoh to bring my people, the Israelites, out of Egypt" (Exodus 3:10). Moses wasn't too thrilled about that. In fact, he tried very hard to talk God out of it. But in the end, he went. The course of redemptive history was changed because Moses got up and went back to Egypt in obedience to God.

What we do in worship and what God does with us is not an insignificant thing. In worship we are dealing with the reality of God's power to transform and change the world. The God who meets the world in its suffering calls us to go into that world as the channel of God's redeeming, liberating love. Genuine worship motivates us for obedient ministry in the world.

I have no idea who first told me that the church in our time is like a professional football game with twenty-two players on the field in need of rest and 80,000 spectators in the stands in need of exercise. Genuine worship, worship that is centered in God's love in Christ, never leaves us as spectators. It motivates us to do something we would not otherwise have done.

One of the most persistent heresies in Christian history is Gnosticism. It's the idea that "spiritual" realities are utterly separate from the ordinary stuff of our human existence. It is always a denial of the Incarnation, a refusal to believe that the Word

> *How does your congregation's experience of worship motivate people to be in ministry in the world?*
>
> *How have you experienced worship that cultivates awareness, ignites awe, energizes compassion, and motivates you for ministry?*

actually became flesh in Jesus Christ. One of the ways Gnosticism continues to affect us is by convincing us that the spiritual life is distinctly separate from tangible, earthly things like our physical bodies. Paul, however, linked the two so tightly together that they are contained in the same sentence. In his letter to Rome, he offered the challenge to "present your bodies as a living sacrifice, holy and acceptable to God, which is your spiritual worship" (Romans 12:1). For Paul, what we do with our bodies and what we do in our worship are inextricably bound together. Offering our bodies in ministry to others is the tangible expression of our worship. The proof of the effectiveness of our worship is not the difference it makes in the lives of people when they are in church, but the difference it makes when they are scattered in the world.

With those four challenges before us, let me share some of the ways we are fulfilling our mission of "Making God's Love Real" in worship at Hyde Park.

First, we make God's love real through worship that glorifies God.

Throughout the Bible, mountains are mysterious places, holy places, places where a person might just run head-on into the presence of God. Whenever someone goes up to the mountains, something important is going to happen. My guess is that if you asked Peter, James, and John, they would say that their greatest experience of worship happened the day Jesus took them up on a high mountain (Luke 9:28-36).

Luke records that "while [Jesus] was praying, the appearance

of his face changed, and his clothes became dazzling white"
(Luke 9:29). Moses and Elijah "appeared in glory and were
speaking of his departure, which he was about to accomplish at
Jerusalem" (9:31). Although the disciples were "weighed down
with sleep," they woke up and "saw his glory." We call that experience of glory "Transfiguration."

In the modern era, most people had a hard time with the
Transfiguration story. Heavily influenced by the Enlightenment
and Western European rationalism, we were pretty much convinced that the only things that are real are things that can be
proved by the scientific process. The result was that we either
wasted a lot of time trying to explain away the mystical elements
in this story or we simply ignored it altogether.

But we don't live in the modern era anymore. We're now in
what is called the postmodern era, which, when you think about
it, doesn't say as much about where we are as where we aren't!
But we're all affected by it. The postmodern mindset is not
imprisoned within the limitations of rationalism and the scientific process. It's much more open to a sense of mystery that
extends beyond the things we can explain in finite, human cate-
gories. Shakespeare was speaking like a true postmodern when
he had Hamlet say,

> There are more things in heaven and earth, Horatio,
> Than are dreamt of in your philosophy.
>
> (*Hamlet,* Act 1, Scene 5)

In the postmodern era, people are more drawn to experience than to rational content and are therefore much more open to experiencing this story. We can't explain *what* happened on the

What does the word "glory" mean to you?

mountain that day, but we know that *something* happened, something that touched the lives of the disciples so deeply that it sent
them back into the ordinary paths of their ordinary lives with an
extraordinary vision planted in their souls. And the word they
used to describe it was "glory."

Luke is a master at painting powerful word pictures. He would have known that the word "glory" came from the Hebrew root, *kabod*, which literally means "weight" or "heaviness." Glory is the weight that measures the inherent value of something. It's what we mean when we measure the value of a diamond by its weight in carats, or we say something is worth its weight in gold. It may be that Luke was painting a bold linguistic contrast between the disciples who were "weighed down with sleep" and Jesus who was bearing the full weight (*kabod*) of the glory of God.

Tom Farmer is the pastor at Saint Paul's United Methodist Church in Largo, Florida. He's a Southern boy whose favorite expression is, "Glory!" When his football team wins, he shouts, "Glory!" I was in his office one time and noticed the word "Glory" sitting on his windowsill. It looked as if it had been cut out of foam. Tom said a guy in the church made it for him. He told me to pick it up. I reached over with one hand to pick up the foam "Glory," but I couldn't lift it. I had to use both hands. It wasn't carved from foam; it was molded in solid lead.

I doubt that the guy who molded the word "glory" for Tom understood Hebrew, but he got it right! In the letter to the Corinthians, Paul talks about the "eternal weight of the glory of God" (2 Corinthians 4:17). The glory of God, revealed in Jesus Christ, is not some light, esoteric, ephemeral triumph over the real pain and problems of life. The glory of God revealed in Jesus is the transfiguring power that never denies the reality of human suffering, but meets us in that human suffering. Glory is the full weight of the infinite love of the Almighty God in human experience. The glory of God in Jesus Christ is heavy—as heavy as a cross. And that, of course, is where the Transfiguration story leads us. Jesus, Moses, and Elijah "were speaking of his departure, which he was about to accomplish at Jerusalem." They were looking toward the cross.

> How does Luke's description of "glory" influence your understanding of worship that glorifies God?

In Matthew, Mark, and Luke, the Transfiguration is the hinge upon which the story swings. It is the point at which the narrative turns away from Jesus' teaching and healing to begin the inexorable journey toward the cross. The Gospel writers are convinced that if you want to know what glory is, you will find it at the cross. You'll know what it means to "glorify" God when you see the very human, broken, suffering Jesus dying in obedient, self-giving love. There, and there alone, we know the full weight of the glory of God.

We believe that "Making God's Love Real" through worship means that our worship always leads us toward an experience of God's glory in the self-giving love revealed at the cross. This does not mean that every sermon includes a reference to the Crucifixion or that every worship service is a reminder of Good Friday. It does mean that beneath, around, and through all of our preparation for worship is the continuing question: How will this experience help people experience the transforming love of God that was made real to us at the cross?

> *How does worship lead your people to the glory of God's self-giving love at the cross?*
>
> *Can people be authentically human in worship in your congregation?*

A cruciform understanding of "glory" also means that we enter into worship with the conviction that it is precisely in our human weakness, suffering, and pain that we are most likely to experience the glory of God. It means that we do everything we can to be genuinely human in worship. There are no "stained glass voices." The worship leaders and preachers sound the same in worship as they do when you meet them on the street. We are not uncomfortable with genuine expressions of emotion. We are totally nonmanipulative in the ways we invite people to respond, but people are free to laugh, clap, and cry. Although we do everything we can to avoid mistakes and blunders that could get in the way of our worship, when they happen (as they often do!), we accept them as a part of humanity. And we never hesitate to bring the real stuff of our experience outside the walls of the church into our experience of praise and prayer.

Second, we make God's love real through worship that celebrates our faith.

There are two critically important words in this element of our mission statement. The first is "celebrate." We plan our worship in the constant reminder that Sunday is always the celebration of the resurrection. Even during Lent, the season of repentance that leads us to Good Friday and the cross, the liturgical tradition counts the forty days of penance *excluding Sundays.* Even in the most somber of seasons, when the church gathers for worship, it gathers to celebrate God's victory over death. In ancient traditions, the church at worship always faced east so that the congregation was always looking with hope toward the rising sun.

I am convinced that one of the reasons worship in so many mainline churches is so deadly is that we have forgotten that worship is a time of celebration. We've managed to accomplish something the writers of the New Testament would have thought to be impossible: we have made the gospel boring. Far too often, we confirm H. L. Mencken's cynical observation that "the chief contribution of Protestantism to human thought is its massive proof that God is a bore" (*New York Public Library Book of Twentieth-Century Quotations*, p. 360).

Sam Keen, writing for the growing spiritual awakening among men, said that if he were asked to diagnose the most common spiritual disease of men in our culture today he would not concentrate on "our lust for power, our insatiable hunger for gadgets, or our habit of repressing women and the poor. I would, rather, focus on our lack of joy. Most of the men I know are decent, serious, and hard-working, and would like to make the world a better place. What they are not is juicy, sensual, and fun" (*Fire in the Belly*, p. 171).

My guess is that the same thing could be said for many of our mainline churches at worship. By and large, church people are good, decent, serious, and hard-working folks. They really want to make the world a better place. They just aren't juicy, sensual (meaning worshiping with all of their senses), or fun. To see them in worship, you might think they were born in pickle season and raised on vinegar. They act as if being a Christian were the same as having a bad case of the flu. But that's not the way it's supposed to be. The central note of the Christian faith is the note of celebration, the shout of praise, the thrill of laughter, the rhythm of joy. Christian worship is the continuation of the angelic announcement, "Do not be afraid; for see—I am bringing you good news of great joy for all the people" (Luke 2:10). We worship in confident assurance of the presence of the Risen Christ who said, "Be of good cheer; I have overcome the world" (John 16:33 KJV).

In planning our worship, we always look for the note of celebration. Every worship service includes a note of joyful gratitude for what God has done in the past and exuberant hope for what God will do in the future. Even on the darkest of days—days when we face the full fury of suffering and death—our music includes an element of praise and affirmation that will send people out on a note of hope. In preparation for preaching, I keep in mind a seminary professor who said that he looked at every sermon for places where it *How is the spirit of celebration expressed in your worship?* "sparkled" with a note of joy. We make God's love real when we celebrate our faith.

The second critically important word in this part of our mission statement is "faith," by which we mean "the faith," the Christian faith that has been handed down to us across the generations, the faith that is expressed in the historic creeds of the church. We didn't make it up. It is not ours to refashion into a religion of our own liking. "The faith" has been entrusted to us. Our task is to celebrate the historic affirmations of the Christian faith in ways that enable spiritually hungry, soulfully searching people to experience their power and live in their truth.

In an earlier book on the Apostles' Creed, I quoted the British dramatist-theologian, Dorothy Sayers, who said:

> The Christian faith is the most exciting drama that ever staggered the imagination of man—and the dogma is the drama. . . . If

we think it dull it is because we either have never really read those amazing documents, or have recited them so often and so mechanically as to have lost all sense of their meaning. . . . We may call that doctrine exhilarating or we may call it devastating; we may call it revelation or we may call it rubbish; but if we call it dull, then words have no meaning at all. (*Creed or Chaos*, pp. 3-7, quoted in *Believe in Me*, p. 11)

Theology matters. In the modern era, it mattered because people were looking for a reasoned and reasonable faith. It matters in the postmodern era because it provides the foundation upon which the experience of worship is built. The difference is that the content comes through the experience, not the other way around. Len Wilson and Jason Moore have been leading the church in discovering how to provide an experience in worship that will reach the "digital" culture in which we live. They affirm that "the purpose of a metaphor in worship is to provide a multi-faceted point of entry by representing the basics of the biblical story in a language that the culture can understand" (*Digital Storytellers: the Art of Communicating the Gospel in Worship*, p. 36).

When we began planning to add a contemporary worship service, we made a clear commitment to the creeds and liturgical tradition of the church. Our goal was to find fresh, new ways to celebrate the historic truths of the Christian faith. We unashamedly follow the liturgical year, we celebrate the sacraments, we affirm the historic faith, but we are constantly looking for creative ways to make those affirmations an experiential reality for spiritually hungry people. We are now in the planning stages for a worship experience designed primarily for Gen-Xers that will push the boundaries on that commitment in a whole new way. The core truths of the faith will remain the

How does your worship affirm the historic faith and traditions that have been passed down to your congregation? How are you translating a cognitive understanding of the faith into experiential reality in your worship?

same, but the form in which they are experienced will be radically different.

Third, we make God's love real through worship that invites others to faith in Christ.

I'll grant that there is no direct evidence that Joseph taught his son to fish, but a quick reading of the Gospels will convince you that Jesus liked hanging around with fishermen. One day as he walked along the shore, he stopped to watch Simon and Andrew "cast a net into the sea—for they were fishermen." That's just what they were. And that's just what Jesus needed. He offered his invitation to them: "Follow me, and I will make you fish for people" (Matthew 4:19).

I grew up on the King James Version of Jesus' invitation, "I will make you fishers of men." The dictionary says that the noun, "fishers," is archaic. We don't talk that way anymore. And, of course, we don't use "men" in the generic sense either. Jesus clearly intended to catch people of both sexes. Still, there's a fascinating linguistic twist there. I checked the original language. Matthew uses exactly the same Greek noun in both places to say "they were fishermen" and, literally, "fishermen of human beings."

Translate it any way you like. Jesus called these fishermen just as they were. He met them in the middle of the real work of their very real lives. He called them in words they could understand. He promised to use them to draw others into the kingdom of God. And just the way he called those fishermen, he calls us to go fishing with him.

It's important to note that before Jesus called his first disciples, he left Nazareth and made his home in Capernaum, which Matthew describes as "Galilee of the Gentiles" (Matthew 4:15). Matthew was doing more than describing geography. Nazareth was a cozy little village of faithful, law-abiding, kosher Jews. Capernaum, on the other hand, was a more cosmopolitan area. Capernaum was filled with non-Hebrew people who were outside the covenant community, unrelated to the Jewish tradition. And Jesus didn't just go for a visit; he settled in, lived among the people, and got to know their world.

Jesus' movement from Nazareth to Capernaum could be a model for us. Like him, we are called to live in a world that is full of people who are unrelated to the gospel—people who do not know the language and traditions of the faith. He calls us to get to know the people in the world around us and to discover how to connect with them.

I was having lunch with a group of pastors a few weeks before Mother's Day. One of the pastors said that a newspaper reporter had called him that week. She was doing an article on family life and wanted to ask him some questions about families in the church. After he answered those questions, she said she wanted to ask some questions about families who were not in the church. He laughed and told us, "I asked her what she expected of me. Everyone I know is in the church." I felt like saying, "You need to get out more!" Without realizing what he had said, he had demonstrated the way the mainline church has largely forgotten that we are called to be a missionary church in a mission situation. Jesus calls us to relate to secular people who are not actively involved in the life of the Kingdom through a local community of faith by learning their language, sharing their lives, experiencing life as they experience it by living among them. As we plan for worship, we are constantly asking ourselves whether the language, music, images, stories, and visuals we are using will be intelligible to people who have not been inside the church before.

> *How effectively does worship in your congregation relate to people who are not already inside the church?*

A pastor friend was standing in the checkout line at the grocery store one morning when he overheard a conversation between the cashier and the woman in front of him. The woman was complaining about all her problems. The cashier listened as she pulled the groceries across that little magic box that totals up the bill. When the cashier finished, she asked the woman, "Do you go to church?" The woman said, "No." The cashier replied, "I go to a great church. It's helped me, and it might help you." The cashier took the woman's receipt and drew a little map on it so the customer could find her way. The woman smiled, thanked her, and walked away.

My friend was impressed by the power of that simple witness. Later that day, he had lunch in a little restaurant where a dark-haired woman waited on him. He made conversation while she served him, and when she brought the check, he surprised himself by asking, "Do you go to church?" The waitress paused and said, "No, but I've been thinking about it." Then she went on, "I'm a single parent and I'm having a tough time getting it all together. I've been thinking about trying to find a church." Modeling the lesson he had learned that morning, he said, "I go to a great church. It's helped me a lot. It might help you." He took his receipt and drew a map for her. The next Sunday, it would have been hard to guess who was more surprised: my friend when he saw the waitress coming toward the church door or the waitress when she found out he was the preacher! As far as I know, she's been there ever since.

In planning for worship, we intentionally look for ways to invite people into faith in Christ. Sometimes that invitation takes the form of a time of guided, silent prayer. Sometimes it means a very specific response of commitment. Sometimes it is as simple as an invitation to indicate on a "Welcome Card" whether the person renewed or made a new

> *How long has it been since you sensed that you were being sent into the world like the shepherd who Jesus said went to find one lost sheep?*
>
> *How long has it been since you invited someone to experience the life and love of God in Jesus Christ?*
>
> *How would an unchurched person feel in your worship service?*

commitment to Christ that day. When we serve Holy Communion, it includes an invitation to pray with one of the pastors about specific needs. Whatever form the invitation takes, making God's love real in worship means inviting spiritually hungry people to taste the bread of life.

So, how do we plan for worship that glorifies God, celebrates the faith, and invites others to faith in Christ?

One of the things I'm learning about "digital" culture from the Gen-Xers in our worship team is a fresh understanding of teamwork. Jason Moore says that "planning worship with the intent of reaching this culture is much too hard to do alone." He's got that right! "The collective ownership of putting together worship in a team makes implementing it much fun" (*Digital Storytellers,* p. 47). It is more fun, and more creative, too, but I'll confess that it's been a big adjustment for a Boomer like me who learned to do it solo! I was accustomed to planning my sermons and giving the themes to music directors who chose anthems to go with them. Beyond that, it was pretty much a process of filling in the blanks on the order of worship. Moving to a more visual, interactive experience in worship has called for insights into the culture, skills in computer technology, and gifts for envisioning the service that no one person could possess.

Across the years we have attempted all sorts of processes to build the worship team, many of which simply didn't work. Finally, under the leadership of our Gen-X Associate Pastor, the Reverend Magrey de Vega, we developed a process that maximizes the individual strengths of each of the people involved in worship while working as teams. The only thing I do alone now is the actual writing of the sermon, but even that task involves interaction with other team members.

A New Worship Planning Model

A. The Goals for Our Worship Planning Process

To maintain and enhance a deep understanding of the true nature of worship and the scriptural roots upon which every service should be based

To restructure the worship staff so that each staff person contributes his or her own unique gifts in ways that best suit his or her individual talents and needs

To plan worship services reasonably well enough in advance so that each service is done with excellence

To involve laypeople more fully in the design and evaluation processes

B. The Planning Teams

Pastoral Staff—consists of the three ordained pastors

Function: To determine the weekly Scripture texts, sketch out upcoming overall series, including series title, and sermon titles. (The group begins with the Revised Common Lectionary, but is not bound to follow it.)

Meets: Informally throughout the year

Outcome: Series, Scriptures, and themes are planned 3-5 months in advance.

Spiritual Direction Team—consists of the senior pastor, associate pastors, director of adult education, church administrator, and lay leaders

Function: To give theological and thematic basis for weekly services based on the Scripture texts, including the felt need, desired outcome, mood/vibe of the service, theme synopsis, and thematic direction

Meets: Once a month for two hours

Outcome: Services are planned 4-8 weeks in advance with information immediately distributed to entire worship staff in printed form.

Creativity Team—consists of the director of media arts, directors of youth and children's ministries, associate pastor responsible for worship planning, lay members of the drama and technical team, Chancel Choir director, and contemporary music director

Function: To translate the theological and thematic content of each service into relevant, creative forms, including music, computer graphics, video, drama, sermon support, and congregational participation/response

Meets: Twice a month for two hours

Outcome: Services are planned 2-3 weeks in advance with information distributed to entire worship staff in printed form.

C. Lay Involvement

PREWORSHIP INSIGHT AND SHARING
The worship ministry coordinator (a lay volunteer) and the two lay leaders are invited to include the weekly scripture lessons into their personal prayer/devotional time. They are asked to share their insights on how the texts speak to our congregation with the Spiritual Direction Team.

POSTWORSHIP EVALUATION
The worship ministry coordinator and the two lay leaders are encouraged to provide feedback to the Worship Team in evaluating how effectively the defined goals of the service were accomplished.

OTHER POSSIBILITIES FOR LAY INVOLVEMENT
We anticipate including a wider range of laypeople in the pre- and postworship process particularly related to the Creativity Team.
    We look toward developing a small group whose primary purpose is the study of the weekly scriptures and whose feedback will be included in the worship planning process.

D. Logistics

PREWORSHIP LOGISTICS
    Definition: Any logistical concerns that affect the worship service

Process: Logistical ideas or concerns that emerge in the Spiritual Direction and Creativity Team meetings are directed to the staff person most directly related to it. The ideas or concerns are discussed in the full staff meetings as we move toward that particular Sunday. On Wednesday afternoon, the entire Worship Team meets to go over details of the service for the weekend ahead.

POSTWORSHIP LOGISTICS

Definition: Any logistical concern that arises as a result of a worship service

Process: The concerned staff person raises the issue by naming and describing it on the white board in the conference room where it can become a part of the evaluation process.

What process do you use in planning your worship services? Does your process reflect your mission?

During a Saturday evening dinner in an outdoor cafe in Dublin, Ireland, with my wife and some friends, I got into conversation with Beth, the bright, attractive young woman who was our waitress. She had grown up in the city and was working part time to put herself through graduate school. When she brought us our dessert, I asked if she knew of a good church in the city. She gave directions to the cathedral and said she thought they gave guided tours of the place. I replied that I wasn't really thinking of a museum-type tour, but a place to attend worship. I asked whether she knew of a church where folks her age might go to worship. It seemed like a foreign concept to her. She said, "No young people I know go to church." She said she didn't know of any church in the city that had young people in it. But then she said, "If you find one, I might be interested."

I've wondered ever since whether there was a church in Dublin that might offer the kind of worship that would relate to Beth and her friends, worship that would go all the way to her

> *How effectively do the worship services in your church accomplish your mission?*
>
> *Are you learning how to offer worship that might connect the historic affirmations of the Christian faith with people who have never heard them before?*
>
> *What changes would need to occur in your worship to reach people like Beth?*

heart. I keep her face in my memory as a challenge for us to create worship that might invite people like her to faith in Christ.

There's a contemporary praise song that we use in our staff prayer time. It says, "I'm going back to the heart of worship, and it's all about you, Jesus." Ultimately, worship that touches the heart is worship that takes us back to Jesus. It's really not about us; it's about God's great love made real among us in the life, death, and resurrection of Jesus and about finding the most effective way to draw people into an experience of that love. It's about getting ourselves out of the way so that God can do something in and through us that will transform and heal our hearts.

CHAPTER 12

Habits for a Healthy Heart

Christian life is learned and lived through the cultivation of specific habits and practices . . . that enable us simultaneously to unlearn our habits of sinfulness.

—L. Gregory Jones, *Embodying Forgiveness*

Here are the questions all heart patients have to answer after they come through a cardiac crisis: What must I do to maintain a healthy heart? What habits and practices do I need to adopt that will strengthen my heart for the long haul? And those are the questions for every transformational leader and every transforming congregation. Congregational cardiology is not a one-time cure. It is an ongoing process of heart transformation that never ends.

Not long ago we spent a considerable amount of time in our ministry staff retreat looking at who we are, how we work together, and where we believe the Spirit is leading us. Partway through the retreat one of our team members said, "I came here thinking that we would work all this stuff out and be done with it. Now I realize that it is a process that won't end. I'm ready to keep on living with it."

Exactly ten years after my cardiac crisis, while I was completing the final draft of this book, it happened again. I woke up one morning and could feel the unmistakable signs of atrial fibrillation. For years my annual checkups were a routine affair that provided little more than an opportunity for a pastoral visit with my church member cardiologist. The previous two years had been two of the healthiest of all my years in Tampa. My asthma had been well controlled. I was walking three miles on the Tampa Bayshore three mornings a week and working out on the exercise machines at the YMCA in the afternoon. I had been managing the unavoidable stress of my work better than ever before. All in all, I felt like a pretty healthy 55-year-old guy with good work to do, a beautiful community in which to do it, a great family, and a first grandchild on the way.

Like most folks, my first reaction was denial. I told myself it was probably just too much caffeine in my system and was sure it would go away. But it didn't stop. In fact, I could feel the rate becoming more irregular as the days went on. When I checked in with my cardiologist, the EKG quickly confirmed that I was in atrial fibrillation. He immediately prescribed blood thinner to prevent the possibility of a stroke along with medications designed to slow down my heart rate. An echocardiogram revealed the good news that there was no damage to the heart muscle or chambers. We decided to wait to see whether it would correct itself or would have to be shocked back into rhythm. The doctor did, in fact, perform a cardio-version, and my heart has been ticking along in perfect rhythm ever since.

The odds are that this recent episode had little or nothing to do with what happened ten years ago. Medically speaking, it's sheer coincidence that it happened when it did; the heart doesn't keep a calendar of anniversaries and couldn't care less that I was writing this book. But this unexpected recurrence of the most common symptom of heart trouble was enough to remind me that the process of maintaining a healthy heart is not something that gets taken care of once and is settled forever. It's a lifelong process involving healthy habits of diet, exercise, and rest.

What habits have you developed to maintain a healthy heart?

In our personal spiritual formation, the process of dying and being raised to new life in Christ is not a one-time event, but an ongoing work of the Spirit of God in the deepest part of our being. In the opening chapter of this book, I quoted L. Gregory Jones who used the continuous present tense when he said that "as we participate in Christ's dying *and* rising, we die to our old selves and find a future not bound by the past." He described "a lifelong practice of living into that baptism, of daily dying to old selves and living into the promise of an embodied new life" (*Embodying Forgiveness*, p. 4, italics his).

Dying and rising again is the ongoing process of self-surrender through which God shapes us into the likeness of Jesus Christ. Paul described the process in the metaphor of childbirth when he told the Galatians, "My little children, for whom I am again in the pain of childbirth until Christ is formed in you" (Galatians 4:19). John Wesley used the term "sanctification," the process by which our hearts are continuously renewed and transformed by the love of God at work within us. It's the process Charles Wesley described when he taught the early Methodists to sing:

> Finish, then, thy new creation;
> Pure and spotless let us be.
> Let us see they great salvation
> Perfectly restored in thee;
> Changed from glory into glory,
> Till in heaven we take our place,
> Till we cast our crowns before thee,
> Lost in wonder, love, and praise.

> (*The United Methodist Hymnal*, no. 384)

I'll never forget a farmer in the little church I served in rural, north central Florida. He didn't have a lot of formal education, but every now and then he would come through with some absolutely brilliant stuff. I'll never forget the day he came up the church steps and I asked, "How you doing today?" He grabbed my hand, looked into my eyes, and said, "Well, Preacher, I'll tell you. I'm not the man I used to be, and I'm not yet the man I'd like to be, but I'm more the man God wants me to be than I've

> *How have you experienced the process of sanctification in your relationship with God? What does the language of "dying and rising again" mean for you?*

ever been before." That's a pretty good description of the process by which God takes us from where we have been, gives us a vision of who we are to become, and then works within us along the way to enable us to become all that God intends for us to be.

Like my major heart crisis a decade ago, there are ways in which I can see my recent episode as a physiological paradigm of the continuing work of transformation in the heart of our congregation with one major difference. Ten years ago, the crisis took us to the heart of our mission and identity. It led us toward clarity about *who* we are and *what* we are called to be. That heart-level understanding of our mission is no longer up for grabs. It is, rather, the baseline of our life together. The continuing process of "dying to old selves and living into the promise" of new life in the congregation revolves around questions of *how* we fulfill that mission in the constantly changing realities of the community and world around us as we grow in obedience to the way and will of Christ.

So, how does a congregation maintain a healthy heart for the long haul? One way to answer that question is to go back to the model of vibrant, healthy, Spirit-energized congregational life recorded in the book of Acts. Luke, the physician, offers his summary diagnosis in Acts 2:43-47 and 4:32-33. Several key elements of healthy congregational life emerge from that passage.

First, the early Christians shared *a common mission*. Luke records: "The whole group of those who believed were of one heart and soul. . . . With great power, the apostles gave their testimony to the resurrection of the Lord Jesus, and great grace was upon them" (Acts 4:32-33).

Faith in the Risen Christ took form in the early church through a clearly defined sense of common mission. They knew why they were there. They were there to declare and experience the grace of God made known in the cross and the resurrection of Jesus

Christ. They were there to invite every human being to experience that same life and grace. The Bible never says that all of the disciples were the same. They weren't! We would hardly have a New Testament at all if there had not been so much difference of opinion, misunderstanding, and confusion about the specific ways in which to accomplish that mission. A whole lot of the New Testament is the result of the early church trying to sort out the differences that existed among the people in those congregations. But at the center is this common mission, a clear sense of why the church was there: to give testimony to the resurrection of the Lord Jesus.

And that's the way we have continued to attempt to live out our mission of "Making God's Love Real." Hyde Park is a very diverse body of people who share a common mission and have made a commitment to accomplish it. Because we were willing to pay the price of going to the heart of our identity in defining our mission and vision, we have a continually growing clarity about why this church is here. We are here to make the love of God revealed in Jesus Christ a tangible reality in the lives of men, women, and children in this community and, extending from this community, around the world. We are here to transform ordinary people into extraordinary lovers of God and of others. Our task is to draw everyone more deeply into the central core of that mission which is the love and grace of God made known in Jesus Christ.

Around the circumference of that mission are a wide variety of very important issues and concerns that clamor for our response. All of them are important, but none of them are central. All of them concern us, but none of them define us. The defining core of our identity is the love and grace of God in Jesus Christ, proclaimed in the Apostles' Creed and experienced through the Wesleyan tradition. That's the center. Everything else is on the circumference. What we are discovering is that the more deeply we are drawn into that central core of faith in Jesus Christ, the more closely we are drawn to each other with all the uniqueness and diversity of our lives. It is from that common center that we attempt to look out to all of the things on the circumference. We are called to struggle together to discover how the Spirit will lead us to apply our understanding of the gospel to each of those specific issues.

That's not always easy. As I complete this manuscript, the United States is seriously considering a second war with Iraq. The people of our congregation represent the whole continuum of conviction from "Christian nonviolence" to the "Just War" theory. Many persons hold their political convictions with all of the political passion that defines itself as patriotism in the wake of 9/11. As pastoral leaders, we have attempted to be both prophets and pastors. We have tried to define our own convictions about Jesus' call to peacemaking while continuing to respect the convictions of people who see things differently. But that combination of clarity of conviction and respect for differences is simply too difficult for some people to handle. Once again, we have seen people leave our congregation because the pastors did not respond to the current crisis in ways that reinforced the generally accepted assumptions about the use of our military might. But for the most part, we have been able to hold together some widely divergent convictions around our central identity and mission.

> *How deeply does your congregation share a common mission? What is at the center of your life together?*

The second thing that Luke tells us about these early Christians is that they participated in *a common discipline.* He describes their life together in Acts 2:46: "Day by day as they spent much time together in the temple. . . ." Let's pause at the words "day by day" to say that living out a common discipline takes time. It takes time for us to develop the processes and disciplines by which new life in Christ takes form among us. It takes time to build trust in Christian friendships. It takes time to peel back the façade of superficial religiosity and touch the real stuff of each other's lives. If God wants a mushroom, God can pop it up overnight. But if God wants a sequoia, even God can't do it quickly. The process of being formed in the image of Christ takes time.

Back to Luke: "Day by day, they spent much time together in the temple, they broke bread at home and ate their food with glad and generous hearts, praising God and having the goodwill of all the people" (Acts 2:46-47). Eugene Peterson paraphrased that verse to say, "They followed a daily discipline of worship in the temple, followed by meals at home and every meal was a celebration, exuberant and joyful as they praised God!" (*The Message*). My guess is that it would do all of our hearts a lot of good to be a part of a community like that!

There is simply no way for new life in Christ to take tangible form in our experience without shared common discipline. Michael Budde and Robert Brimlow, in *Christianity Incorporated: How Big Business Is Buying the Church*, cut across many unspoken assumptions of twentieth-century church life when they said that "the process of forming Christians has never been automatic, easy, or flawless. . . . There is nothing natural or innate about being a Christian." They compare becoming a Christian disciple to learning a trade or a foreign language. "It requires disciplined apprenticeship under the guidance of others who have internalized the competencies, nuances, and satisfactions attendant to a trade done well or a language rendered eloquently" (Quoted in *Context*, May 1, 2002, p. 3).

We know what the disciplines are for us as a congregation. Having come through this book, you know them, too. Since this book has already described some of the ways we live out those disciplines, let me simply list them here again and ask some questions about them.

The discipline of worship. Just like these first Christians, we are discovering that healthy congregational life is centered in worship—the corporate discipline of gathered worship and the personal discipline of spiritual formation and prayer. Luke says that the people in this rapidly growing community "devoted themselves to . . . the breaking of bread and the prayers" (Acts 2:42).

> *How healthy is your discipline of worship and prayer? What can you do to improve the quality of the sacramental life of your congregation?*

The discipline of education. According to Luke, the early Christians "devoted themselves to the apostles' teaching" (Acts 2:42). People often ask what specific

> *How's your life as a learner? Are you experiencing continual growth as a disciple of Jesus Christ?*

program or ministry has made the biggest difference in our congregation. My answer is always DISCIPLE Bible study. This intensive study of Scripture has become the biblical core of our life together. In addition, we are continuously encouraging people to be lifelong learners through Sunday school classes, short-term studies, and Wesley groups. We are finding that when people are united around the Scripture, God transforms their lives.

The discipline of caring. The love of God in Christ takes form

> *How's your "caring quotient"? Are the pastors of your congregation expected to fulfill the caring needs of the congregation? How are laypersons in your church demonstrating their care for each other?*

in us when we learn to care for other people in tangible and practical ways. We know it's working when the pastors go to the hospital and find a patient surrounded by caring laypeople. We know it's working when the pastors are the last persons to arrive to celebrate the birth of a child or the death of a loved one. The caring mission of the church is fulfilled through caring persons who express God's love for each other.

The discipline of witness and service. Faith in the Risen Christ is never fully realized in us until it takes form in giving ourselves to others through practical forms of witness

> *Are people in your congregation discovering their gifts and using them in ministry? In what measurable ways is your congregation expressing its witness for Christ in the community? Are the people of your church finding practical ways to give themselves away to others in service?*

and of service. It is absolutely essential to healthy spiritual life. For too many generations, American Protestant church people were taught that being a faithful church member meant "sitting" on a committee. And that's exactly what most of them did: they sat! One of the hopeful signs of change in the next generation is that people are no longer measuring their commitment by how many committee meetings they attend, but by how they find ways to serve other people in the name of Christ.

Those four elements of our mission statement define the common discipline that will sustain our congregation for the long haul. We believe that they are nonnegotiable essentials to a healthy spiritual life. They are the practical ways in which we are attempting to maintain a healthy heart.

The third thing Luke tells us about the early Christians is that they demonstrated *a common generosity.* In Acts 2:44-45, he tells us that "all who believed were together and had all things in common; they would sell their possessions and goods and distribute the proceeds to all, as any had need." The same picture emerges in Acts 4:32-35: "No one claimed private ownership of any possessions, but everything they owned was held in common. . . . There was not a needy person among them, for as many as owned lands or houses sold them and brought the proceeds of what was sold. They laid it at the apostles' feet, and it was distributed to each as any had need."

Luke describes a form of communal economics that did not last very long in the New Testament and has never been successfully accomplished on a large scale in this world. But beneath that early Christian communal economy, there is a common level of generosity, a profound awareness that nothing we own belongs to us. As baptized disciples, as followers of a Risen Christ, it all belongs to our Risen Lord. It is his, not ours. We are called to use it in ways that are consistent with his mission and purpose.

A congregation that sustains a healthy heart for the long haul is

How's the generosity level in your congregation? Is there a joyful spirit of generosity in the giving of your people?

a community of people who take Jesus seriously when he said, "Where your treasure is, there will your heart be also." It's a community of people who practice the biblical discipline of tithing as a way of ordering their lives around their commitment to Christ. It's a congregation that openly, freely, and joyfully develops a sense of warmhearted generosity that is something like the extravagant generosity of God.

The first Christians also experienced *the uncommon power of the Spirit of God.* Luke describes it in dramatic terms: "Awe came upon everyone, because many signs and wonders were being done by the apostles" (Acts 2:43). "With great power the apostles gave their testimony to the resurrection of the Lord Jesus, and great grace was upon them" (4:33).

Here's a question to measure the power of the Spirit at work in your congregation: What is happening in your congregation that cannot be explained by anything other than the power of the Spirit of God? If everything that happens in the church can be explained in terms of human effort, human planning, human initiative, and human wisdom, then the future of the church is dependent on the people within it. But when God is at work within a community of people who are sensitive to the power of the Holy Spirit, the total is always equal to more than the sum of the parts. The power of the Spirit takes all of our human efforts and does something with them that goes beyond our human ability to predict, plan, or control.

One of my heroes in the book of Acts is a Jewish rabbi named Gamaliel. Here's the way Luke tells his story in Acts 5:33-39.

> When they heard this, they were enraged and wanted to kill them. But a Pharisee in the council named Gamaliel, a teacher of the law, respected by all the people, stood up and ordered the men to be put outside for a short time. Then he said to them, "Fellow Israelites, consider carefully what you propose to do to these men. For some time ago Theudas rose up, claiming to be somebody, and a number of men, about four hundred, joined him; but he was killed, and all who followed him dispersed and disappeared. After him Judas the Galilean rose up

at the time of the census and got people to follow him; he also perished, and all who followed him were scattered. So in the present case, I tell you, keep away from these men and let them alone; because if this plan or this undertaking is of human origin, it will fail; but if it is of God, you will not be able to overthrow them—in that case you may even be found fighting against God!"

As I look back across the long history of the congregation I serve, I know that if its life had been a thing of human origin and design, it surely would have failed. And as I look back across the transformation that God has been working among us in the past decade, I know that if it had been a human project, it never would have survived. The evidence of God's presence among us is that the undertaking in this congregation, the direction in which this church is moving, was born out of prayer. It is a gift of the uncommon power of God at work among us.

> *How has the life of your congregation experienced the uncommon power of the Spirit of God? What are you doing that could not be done without God's power at work within you?*

CHAPTER 13

A Heart for the Future

For [visionary] companies, the critical question is "How can we do better tomorrow than we did today?" They institutionalize this question as a way of life—a habit of mind and action. . . . In short, it means doing everything possible to make the company stronger tomorrow than it is today.
—James C. Collins and Jerry I. Porras, *Built to Last*

While we were still in college, the young woman who would later become my wife gave me a copy of *Markings*, the spiritual reflections of Dag Hammarskjöld, the formative leader of the United Nations who died in a plane crash in 1961. Two lines from that book hooked my soul back then and have stuck with me ever since.

> For all that has been—Thanks!
> To all that shall be—Yes!
> (*Markings*, p. 89)

Across the years since I first read Hammarskjöld's words, I've come to the conclusion that in those two lines he described the essence of living a healthy, faithful life. It's a bold statement that combines gratitude for the past with confidence for the future. For all that has been—for all the things that have shaped us, all the things that have built us up, all the things that have tried to tear us down, all the influences that have made us who we are—

we say, Thanks! And to all that shall be—to all those promises that are yet to be fulfilled, the expectations that are yet to be realized, the hopes that energize us for the future—we say, Yes!

Looking back on my cardiac crisis, I do not remember feeling fear at the possibility of death. I remember deep feelings of sadness for what I might miss and for those I'd leave behind, but I thank God that I never had any fear of death itself. What I remember most clearly is an overwhelming sense of gratitude for the life I had been given to live and for the people with whom I had been privileged to live it. The things I had done, the places I had gone, the people God led into my life—they all seemed to be an amazing and undeserved gift of God's extravagant generosity to me. Years later, I would remember that feeling when I stood beside the bed of Waller McCleskey just before he died. He was 82 years old. He knew his heart wouldn't keep beating much longer. But I will never forget the smile on his face and the sound of his voice when he said, "It's been a great life!" (I told Waller's story in *Passion, Power, and Praise*, pp. 167-68.)

> *Tell the truth: Are you afraid of death? How do you feel about the prospect of the end of your life?*

When I track the path my life has taken, I find myself singing with the psalmist, "The boundary lines have fallen for me in pleasant places; I have a goodly heritage" (Psalm 16:6). Having faced the very real possibility of death, I've tried to live with a profound sense of gratitude for every gift of God's grace in my life.

The psalmist celebrated God's goodness in the gift of friendship. I love Eugene Peterson's paraphrase of Psalm 16:6: "These God-chosen lives all around—what splendid friends they make!" When I track boundary lines of my journey, I thank God for the friends who have been the gift of God's grace in my life. Frederick Buechner wrote, "You can survive on your own. You can grow strong on your own. You can even prevail on your own. But you cannot become human on your own" (*The Sacred Journey*, p. 46). Those God-chosen friends were with me through my cardiac crisis, and they have been with me all along the way. They have helped me become a real human being.

When I turned fifty, my wife threw a surprise birthday celebration for me at a beach front condominium on the Atlantic coast. The surprise was that she invited all my "clergy cronies," the fellow pastors with whom I have shared my life and ministry. One of them has been a friend for more than thirty years. With the sound of the waves in the background, we ate, drank, and laughed the evening away. At one point I found myself standing alone at one side of the room, looking around at the amazing people God had brought into my life, simply overwhelmed by the gift of their friendship. One of the friends stepped over to me and said, "Jim Harnish, you are a very rich man!" He was correct. I sing with the psalmist, "Therefore, my heart is glad!"

When I thank God for all that has been, I also give thanks that when the call came, we had the good sense to say, Yes. Being a part of God's work of congregational cardiology at Hyde Park continues to be as exhilarating as it is exhausting. I am overwhelmed with gratitude for the awesome joy of sharing the life of this church at this *kairos* moment in its history.

> *How do you feel as you track the lines your life has followed? What good gifts has God brought to you along the way?*

I heard about a young girl who came to her mother one day and said, "You know that heirloom vase that has been handed down in our family from generation to generation? Well, this generation just dropped it!" The longer I am a part of the life of Hyde Park Church, the more grateful I become for the spiritual heritage that has been passed down, generation by generation through the life of this church. In each generation, there have been high moments of great vision and growth and there have been moments of disappointment and near despair. Each generation has reshaped and adapted that spiritual heritage to meet the needs and challenges of its time. I stand in amazement that we get to be a part of the passing on of that spiritual heritage in a time of radical change and growth. But because I believe the

Apostles' Creed when it affirms "the communion of the saints," I have a deep confidence that those who have gone before us are cheering us on as we prepare this congregation for ministry to the next generation.

Hammarskjöld did not only speak of gratitude for the past. He also offered a bold affirmation for the future: "To all that shall be—Yes!"

One of the gifts of grace that God offers to everyone who walks the way that leads through death to life is a renewed commitment to the future. I learned this lesson from my father, in our last visit before his death. He was only fifty-nine years old. By all odds, he should have had many more years of productive living. But the cancer that had begun in his lungs moved to his brain. He faced his death with an honesty that simply amazed the people around him. When I went to Pennsylvania to see him, I took along the architect's drawings for the first building for St. Luke's United Methodist Church. He had made one trip to Orlando and had seen the vacant field covered with palmetto and scrub pine upon which we would one day build a church. We sat together with the plans spread across his hospital table, talking together about how it would be. Finally, he said, "Gee, I wish I could live long enough to see this." He paused for a moment. Then he went on, "But I guess that's how it always is. I guess there is always something you'd like to live a little longer to see."

The truth is that not everyone—and not every church—has that kind of vision for the future. Some people and some congregations become so bound up in their past that they can no longer see the future. They are like Paul D, the former slave in Toni Morrison's novel, *Beloved*. The narrator tells us that he has a "tobacco tin buried in his chest where the red heart used to be. Its lid rusted shut." He tells Sethe, the central character in the story, "me and you, we got more yesterday than anybody. We need some kind of tomorrow" (Quoted in *Embodying Forgiveness*, p. 280). There are people and there are congregations with tin hearts, rusted shut. They live as if they have more yesterdays than tomorrows. They act as if every day is Holy Saturday, the day Christ lay in the tomb. They live—if that word can be used to describe their existence—as if they have never heard the angel at the empty tomb say, "He is going ahead of you" (Mark 16:7). But people of faith, people who have a heart for God's vision of the future, are always looking ahead. There's always more they would like to be able to see.

These are challenging days in which to offer a confident "Yes" to the future, but the church is called to bear witness to hope that is grounded in our faith in God. Ordinary people are drawn together in the Body of Christ because we believe that the heart of God has been revealed in the life, death, and resurrection of Jesus and because we dare to hope that the same God who was present among us in the human Jesus is now at work among us by the power of the Holy Spirit. At the heart of the

> *What do you look forward to seeing in the future? Do you believe that your congregation has more tomorrows than yesterdays?*

church's life is the word of life that is found only when we are willing to die for the right things. It's the kind of faith Paul describes when he reminds the Roman Christians of Abraham, "the father of us all," who trusted in "the God . . . who gives life to the dead and calls into existence the things that do not exist" (Romans 4:17).

The biblical model for visionary faith is Abraham. He was ninety-nine years old. His wife Sarah was no spring chicken either. They were childless, which in that culture meant that they had no future. They had no hope for existence beyond their present moment. There was nothing in front of them to give them hope for the future. Then one day the promise came from God that they were to be the parents of many generations. It was preposterous. The promise was so outlandish, so far beyond their human possibilities that they laughed in the face of God. They laughed, the Genesis writer says, until they rolled on the floor. But when their son was born, they named him Isaac, which means "God laughed." God got the last laugh when the very thing that by all human standards was utterly impossible was the promise that was fulfilled (Genesis 17). Paul said that Abraham was "hoping against hope. . . . No distrust made him waver concerning the promise of God, but he grew strong in his faith as he gave glory to God, being fully convinced that God was able to do what he had promised" (Romans 4:18-21).

Visionary faith holds onto the promise of God even when every human reality seems to be stacked against it, confident that God will accomplish what God has promised. It is faith that believes God is able to bring life out of death. It is a heart-level relationship with God that enables us to look the future in the face and say, Yes!

I was in a small group that was studying the creeds. We came to the affirmation that we believe "in the final triumph of righteousness." The discussion began with a sort of laundry list of all the ways righteousness seems to be taking a beating in the world around us. That led to some conversation about the book of Revelation and the vision of the fulfillment of God's saving purpose at the end of history. After the class, a guy stopped me and said, "Jim, I still don't get it. Tell me in one sentence what the Revelation is all about." I said, "It's right there in the creed: I believe in the final triumph of righteousness. We believe that ultimately God's saving promise will be fulfilled in the whole creation. God's goodness will triumph over every form of evil, and Christ will be Lord of all." He looked me straight in the eye and asked, "Do you really believe that?" I said, "Yep, I really believe that." Then he said, "Then we have a lot of work to do!"

Our work is to do everything in our power to use the resources of the past to energize the congregation in the present and to build into the ongoing life of this congregation those processes of healthy, spiritual growth that will prepare it for ministry in the future.

> *What is the work to which God is calling you and your congregation? What will it mean for you to say "Yes!" to the future of your church?*

But here's the word of warning. It never gets easy. It gets better, but it never gets easy. Collins and Porras discovered that one of the marks of visionary companies is that "they are not exactly comfortable places. . . . They thrive on discontent. They understand that contentment leads to complacency, which inevitably leads to decline" (*Built to Last*, pp. 186-87). James Russell Lowell wrote:

> New occasions teach new duties,
> Time makes ancient good uncouth;
> They must upward still and onward,
> Who would keep abreast of truth.
>
> ("Once to Every Man and Nation,"
> *Pilgrim Hymnal* [Boston: Pilgrim Press,
> 1958], no. 441)

The "new occasion" of life in the aftermath of September 11, 2001, has been teaching us new duties in fulfilling the mission of the church. I've already alluded to the differences of conviction within our church family in regard to a war with Iraq. By the time this book hits the shelves, history will have recorded its verdict on the decisions that are currently being made in Washington, but the underlying difference in biblical interpretation and conviction will remain. For the most part, we are discovering how to "speak the truth in love" and search together for what it will mean for us to fulfill our mission in light of the cultural shifts that have occurred around us. This "winter of discontent" is once again forcing us to go into the heart of our life together. Once again we are learning that for something new to be born, something old within us has to die.

How have changes in the world changed your congregation's understanding of its mission?

The final word for this book must be a word of joy. Through the process of congregational cardiology, we are learning again that the way of costly obedience is the only way to joy. It's the kind of joy the writer of the epistle to the Hebrews proclaimed when he described Jesus as "the pioneer and perfecter of our faith, who for the sake of the joy that was set before him endured the cross" (Hebrews 12:2).

Ezekiel's vision of divine cardiology with which I began this book contains the promise of a joyful fulfillment of God's desire for health and wholeness for the covenant people.

> A new heart I will give you, and a new spirit I will put within you; and I will remove from your body the heart of stone and give you a heart of flesh. I will put my spirit within you, and make you follow my statutes and be careful to observe my ordinances. Then you shall live in the land that I gave to your ancestors; and you shall be my people, and I will be your God. I will save you from all your uncleannesses, and I will summon the grain and make it abundant and lay no famine upon you. I will make the fruit of the tree and the produce of the field abundant, so that you may never again suffer the disgrace of famine among the nations. . . . Then the nations that are left all around you shall know that I, the LORD, have rebuilt the ruined places, and replanted that which was desolate; I, the LORD, have spoken, and I will do it. (Ezekiel 36:26-36)

Every story I know of congregational cardiology has a cross in it. Somewhere along the way to new life, we come through a place of pain, loss, or disappointment. Ultimately, the process always leads to the surrender of our will into the will of God. Something old has to die within us so that something new can be born.

I experienced a significant amount of pain during the Lenten season of 2003. I think it started while I was out of town for a preaching assignment. I went to the YMCA one afternoon and worked out on machines that were different from the ones I use at home. My guess is that I used one of them incorrectly and strained something in my lower back. Back home, I kept working out, thinking the pain would go away, but I finally ended up seeing a physical therapist. My twin brother says that's what I get for exercising in the first place!

At the same time that I was wrestling with back pain, we were wrestling with profound differences within the nation and within our congregation over the prospect of a "pre-emptive" war in Iraq. In the early days of the global debate about what to do in

Iraq, I joined the ordained deacon on our church staff and former Hyde Park pastor, Bishop J. Lloyd Knox (retired) in an interdenominational prayer vigil for peace at the gates of Macdill Air Force Base, the Tampa home of U.S. Central Command. This public witness of peace was painfully disturbing for some of our people.

Always looking for the lesson (or potential sermon illustration!) that the Spirit might teach in times like this, I became aware of two principles about physical exercise that have almost direct parallels to personal and congregational growth.

First, just because we're trying to do the right thing doesn't mean that we won't experience pain. Exercise is a good thing, but it's also very easy to do a small thing in a way that results in pain. Sometimes it's difficult to pin down exactly when and how the pain began, but there's no question about it being there. The movement toward healing always involves acknowledging our pain—pain in our own lives, pain in the lives of others, or pain that we unintentionally cause in others—and dealing with it.

Regarding the conflict in Iraq, the pastors of our congregation had attempted to consistently lift up our understanding of the gospel vision of peace, to pray that our leaders would find a nonviolent resolution to the tension, to support in prayer the men and women of the armed services, and to affirm our respect for brothers and sisters in Christ who saw the conflict differently than we did. While this approach was affirmed by the majority of the people in our congregation, it stirred discomfort in others. Discussions that had been going on at a personal level finally came to the Staff-Parish Relations Committee at their meeting on the Monday of Holy Week.

In a manner that bore witness to the core values and mission of our congregation, the committee members listened to and entered into dialogue with persons who strongly disagreed with the leadership the pastors were giving. They helped us see some ways in which our attempts to live within the prophetic vision of the Scripture had been interpreted by some of our people as being politically, rather than biblically, motivated and helped us understand more deeply the pain within our congregation. As a result, they helped us take some steps toward reconciliation, while still affirming the integrity of our convictions. It was another reminder that pain is an inevitable part of growth. The only way to find healing is to face the pain.

The second principle I learned from my experience with back pain is physically questionable but spiritually accurate. Our high school physical education coach used to say, "No pain. No gain." It's not necessarily true that healthy exercise always produces pain. But, as I learned from the physical therapist, it is true that once an injury has happened, the process of healing will probably be painful. When the physical therapist was stretching my muscles, I began to think that he had been trained to find the place that hurt and make it hurt even worse!

Our natural tendency is to avoid places of pain. The world offers us a multitude of ways to anesthetize the hurt in our lives. But the cross teaches us that the only place of healing is the place of pain. Jesus showed us that the only way to new life is the way that leads through death. To tremble in the darkness of Good Friday is to know that the place of pain is the place where God's love is most fully and clearly made known. If we short-circuit, or deny the pain, we miss out on the deeper work of healing that the Spirit of God can do within and among us. If we bypass Good Friday, we never know the full joy of Easter morning. The only way to life is the way that leads through death. But it is also the way that leads to great joy!

Charles Wesley wrote a hymn that describes the work of divine cardiology in a profound and practical way.

> O for a heart to praise my God,
> A heart from sin set free,
> A heart that always feels thy blood
> So freely shed for me.
>
> A heart resigned, submissive, meek,
> My great Redeemer's throne,
> Where only Christ is heard to speak,
> Where Jesus reigns alone.

A heart in every thought renewed
And full of love divine,
Perfect and right and pure and good,
A copy, Lord, of thine.

Thy nature, gracious Lord, impart;
Come quickly from above;
Write thy new name upon my heart,
Thy new, best name of Love.

(*The United Methodist Hymnal,* no. 417)

The past and the future came together for me one evening when I was stopped on the parking lot by a young couple who were coming from one of our Wesley groups. They had just moved into their first home in South Tampa. They were excited about the church, excited about their small group, excited about what God was doing in their lives. At one point the young husband said that when he realized all they had learned or discovered so far, he couldn't wait to keep studying the Bible and growing together. They said they wanted to know more about tithing their income. Frankly, it's not a question I receive very often, but one I'm always glad to answer!

As we talked, I thought of Waller McCleskey, in part because Waller believed in tithing, in part because I was just beginning to absorb both the pain and the sacred beauty of his death the day before. It hit me that this young couple was just about the age Waller and his wife Doris were when they first came to this church, nearly fifty years earlier, as a young family who had just moved into a new home in Tampa.

I knew that this young couple would never know Waller, so I told them about him. I told them about the simple, quiet, genuine reality of his Christian faith. I told them about how he loved this church and about the way he loved his pastors. I told them about a marriage which for fifty-nine years was the fulfillment of everything that God intended when God thought up the idea of marriage. I told them about our last conversation on the morning he died. Waller said, "I sure would like to see that building completed." And because we believe in the communion of the saints, I said, "Waller, I believe you will." He said, "Yes, I know I will." Finally, I told them about the way he turned to Doris, less than an hour before his last breath. He asked, "How much longer do I have?" She said, "Only the Lord knows that." And he said, "It's been a great life."

I told this young couple, "Now, *that's* why this church is here. This church is here to produce people like that. We're here to begin as early as possible in a person's life, we hope, at their birth, to help them build that kind of marriage, raise that kind of family, develop that kind of faith, and die with that kind of faith. We're here to produce people who can come to the end and look back on their journey and say, 'It's been a great life.'"

As they walked away, I could not help thinking that someday, perhaps fifty years from now, some pastor who is a toddler in some church nursery today, will stand on this same corner, telling another young couple who has just moved into their first home in Tampa, about that young couple, just the way I told them about Waller.

Looking back across the journey we've taken, I can say that the new life that continues to emerge from the process is more than worth the price that was paid. The pain of the difficult years has already been totally overbalanced by the joy of seeing the new life that God is bringing forth among us. The path of obedience always leads to joy! For God's sake, for your congregation's sake, for your own sake, don't settle for anything less!

New Hope
for Mainline Churches:
God Isn't Finished with Us Yet

The reports on the decline of the old-line, formerly mainline, now often sideline Protestant denominations are as redundant as they are depressing. The cultural dominance through which they influenced American culture until the middle of the last century is now a distant memory. My own denomination, The United Methodist Church, has been in steady numerical decline since the day The Methodist Church and the Evangelical United Brethren Church merged to form it in 1968. We still count our "good" years as those years in which our rate of membership decline is less than the previous one. From an institutional perspective, we heirs of the Methodist tradition have good reason for despair, although our denominational leaders have been unusually effective in living in near total denial of our condition.

It's not as if there is anything terribly unique about either the statistics of decline or the power of denial within United Methodism. They are, in fact, typical of the decline and denial in nearly all of America's mainline, Protestant denominations. Today less than 50 percent of all church-going Americans worship in mainline churches, while independent Christian congregations are exploding and the Mormons have grown by an average of 43 percent per decade across the twentieth century. Episcopal Bishop Claude E. Payne and Hamilton Beazley came to the conclusion that "denial about the seriousness of the disease afflicting the Church pervades every level of the mainline denominations" (*Reclaiming the Great Commission*, pp. 7, 27).

In spite of the disturbing trends, my conviction is that God may not be finished with us yet! My experience is that there is a massive population of spiritually searching people who still find within the center flow of the Methodist tradition an understanding of the Christian faith that is the most appropriate framework for their Christian experience. When they hear the gospel in the context of our tradition, their immediate response is something like, "Where have you been all my life?" I suspect that the same is true for the other mainline Christian traditions as well. Although I am quite sure that God is not dependent on the survival of our denominations for the kingdom of God to come on earth as it is in heaven, I'm also confident that to the degree to which we allow it to happen, the Spirit of God can still use the resources, spiritual tradition, and identity of mainline, denominational congregations in the transformation of the world.

If the mainline denominations are to once again become a Spirit-energized movement that will have a transforming influence in our culture, a significant part of that ministry will need to happen through older congregations that receive a new heart for witness and ministry in the future. Another of Ezekiel's physiological visions may yet be fulfilled in us: these dry bones can live again! (Ezekiel 37:1-14).

Some of the most disturbing words Jesus ever spoke are recorded in Matthew 21:43: "Therefore I tell you, the kingdom of God will be taken away from you and given to a people that produces the fruits of the kingdom." God's kingdom vision will be fulfilled; a spiritually hungry world will be fed. The question is whether we in the mainline churches will provide a banquet table, or whether people will have to turn elsewhere.

Based on their experience of renewal within the Episcopal Church, Bishop Claude E. Payne and Hamilton Beazley declare their confidence that "if the Christian community can recover its sense of being God's agent for transformation, and if it can recover its passion for making disciples, it can reach out to the spiritually hungry and offer them the rich banquet of the Christian life." They share with others the concern that "the spiritual hunger in America, like any other kind of hunger, will be satisfied one way or another, or the hungry will die. Spiritually hungry people can feast at the table . . . or they can make do with the spiritual equivalent of junk food, offered by whoever holds out the first morsel" (*Reclaiming the Great Commission*, p. 13). Spiritually starving people will find food. It's time for clergy and lay leaders to decide whether we are willing to be used by God to meet that hunger out of the rich resources of the Christian tradition. Either we will choose to become a productive part of the new thing God is doing in our world or God will find someone else to do it. Now is the time for us to decide.

Those of us who serve in the mainline denominations may sometimes feel like the Old Testament prophet, Nehemiah. The king asked him, "Why is your face sad, since you are not sick? This can only be sadness of the heart." Nehemiah replied, "Why should my face not be sad, when the city, the place of my ancestors' graves, lies in waste, and its gates have been destroyed by fire?" Some of us feel that same sadness of heart when we see once vital congregations now moving toward decline and eventual death. When the king asked Nehemiah what he wanted, Nehemiah replied, "I ask that you send me to Judah, to the city of my ancestors' graves, so that I may rebuild it" (Nehemiah 2:2-5). And that's what Nehemiah did. He went back to rebuild the city.

Adam Hamilton leads The United Methodist Church of the Resurrection, which is one of the most rapidly growing congregations in America. He lifts up the hopeful conviction that "the next great awakening in American Christianity will happen among the historic mainline denominations" (*Leading Beyond the Walls*, p. 203). If he is correct (and I hope he is!) it may well be that God is calling prophetic spiritual leaders to rebuild the congregations of their ancestors so that they become a living expression of the kingdom of God that was revealed in Jesus and is being formed among us by the Holy Spirit. In that calling, no simplistic, superficial makeovers or organizational tinkering will do. It's a process of transformation that goes all the way to the heart. My hope and prayer is that lay and pastoral leaders in long-established, mainline congregations will experience a work of divine congregational cardiology that will energize their congregations for life-transforming, Kingdom-shaped ministry to their communities. If the story of the work of God among us makes a helpful contribution to that transformation, we will be very grateful!

Resources for Congregational Cardiology

Bandy, Thomas G. *Kicking Habits: Welcome Relief for Addicted Churches*. Nashville: Abingdon Press, 1997.

————. *Moving Off the Map: A Field Guide to Changing the Congregation*. Nashville: Abingdon Press, 1998.

Chesterton, G. K. *Orthodoxy: The Romance of Faith*. New York: Doubleday, 1990.

Chestnut, Robert A. *Transforming the Mainline Church*. Louisville: Geneva Press, 2000.

Collins, James C. and Jerry I. Porras. *Built to Last: Successful Habits of Visionary Companies*. New York: HarperBusiness, 1994.

Collins, Jim. *Good to Great*. New York: Harper Business, 2001.

Dudley, Carl S. and Nancy T. Ammerman. *Congregations in Transition: A Guide for Analyzing, Assessing, and Adapting in Changing Communities*. San Francisco: Jossey-Bass Publication, 2002.

Easum, William M. *Sacred Cows Make Gourmet Burgers*. Nashville: Abingdon Press, 1995.

Gomes, Peter. *The Good Book*. New York: William Morrow, 1996.

Hamilton, Adam. *Leading Beyond the Walls*. Nashville: Abingdon Press, 2002.

Hammarskjöld, Dag. *Markings*. New York: Alfred A. Knopf, 1966.

Harnish, James A. *Journey to the Center of the Faith: An Explorer's Guide to Christian Living*. Nashville: Abingdon Press, 2001.

————. *Passion, Power, and Praise: A Model for Men's Spirituality from the Life of David*. Nashville: Abingdon Press, 2000.

Herrington, Jim, Mike Bonem, and James Harold Furr. *Leading

Congregational Change: A Practical Guide for the Transformational Journey. San Francisco: Jossey-Bass Publication, 2000.

Jones, L. Gregory. *Embodying Forgiveness*. Grand Rapids: William B. Eerdmans Publishing Company, 1995.

Mead, Loren B. *The Once and Future Church: Reinventing the Congregation for a New Mission Frontier*. Washington, D.C.: The Alban Institute, 1991.

Nelson, Alan and Gene Appel. *How to Change Your Church (Without Killing It)*. Nashville: W Publishing Group, 2000.

Norris, Kathleen. *Amazing Grace: A Vocabulary of Faith*. New York: Riverhead Books, 1998.

Payne, Claude E. and Hamilton Beazley. *Reclaiming the Great Commission*. San Francisco: Jossey-Bass Publication, 2000.

Rendle, Gilbert R. *Leading Change in the Congregation*. Washington, D.C.: The Alban Institute, 1998.

Storey, Peter. *With God in the Crucible*. Nashville: Abingdon Press, 2002.

Weems, Lovett H. Jr. *Leadership in the Wesleyan Spirit*. Nashville: Abingdon Press, 1999.

Wills, Dick. *Waking to God's Dream*. Nashville: Abingdon Press, 1999.

Wilson, Len and Jason Moore. *Digital Storytellers: The Art of Communicating the Gospel in Worship*. Nashville: Abingdon Press, 2002.

"We have a lot of literature on church growth and church planting. Here is a different kind of story—a remarkable one—that needs to be heard. Thousands of churches in the United States need the kind of transformation Hyde Park has experienced. This book will not only inspire, it will inform and equip pastors and laypersons for the work of the renewal of existing congregations. This is one of our greatest needs today."

Maxie D. Dunnam, President, Asbury Theological Seminary

"Jim Harnish has provided us with a very personal story of his own recovery from a heart attack and his subsequent discoveries about 'congregational cardiology.' Written in very readable story form, drawing upon his vast experience of ministry in a variety of settings, and focusing upon the revitalization of Hyde Park United Methodist Church in Tampa, Florida, under his leadership, Jim has gifted all of us with new insights about how 'the heart of the matter is always a matter of heart.' The book provides diagnosis and hope for a full recovery for pastors, lay leaders, and all who desire to see mainline churches reborn. But be warned, Jim's story and this book teaches us that the way to new life is through the death of our old ways."

Michael J. Coyner, Bishop of the Dakotas Area of The United Methodist Church

---

"In a culture that too readily seeks the quick fix, the magical formula, or the hottest new program idea, Jim Harnish shares with us the unvarnished and grace-filled truth: Success involves honesty, imagination, hard work, faithfulness, laughter, and prayer. It involves the risky business of establishing new priorities of the heart. Harnish is an 'encourager'; he literally 'gives heart' to those of us who believe old congregations can find new life and purpose. In these pages one is able to glance over the shoulder of a fine pastor and glimpse into his soul and mind as he reflects on this 'heart work' of congregational renewal and encouragement. Fortunately, this is not a unique story. From Boston to Denver to San Francisco there are signs of restoration and vitality for oldline congregations. Still, these stories are rare enough that we are fortunate to have a scribe of Harnish's talent to share his personal and communal odyssey with us.

"In this volume we read of the unadorned and challenging truth that congregations can successfully move from being rich in legacy to being a people rich in faith for Christ and for God's reign on earth. As Harnish so aptly puts it, 'Hope is born when we are willing to die for the right things.' In such faithful work it is love and laughter that provide the map and the fuel for the journey. There is little time for the parsing of doctrinal distinctions or the championing of idiosyncratic causes. The reader will discover many practical insights, but more than all else this book demonstrates that the 'heart work' that truly renews a congregation centers in the mystery of love and the imagination of the faithful."

Philip A. Amerson, President and Professor of Church and Society,
The Claremont School of Theology

"Harnish has written a theologically sound, practical guide to congregational health. Drawing on a variety of helpful resources, including his own extensive personal and pastoral experience, this creative and committed pastor provides a convincing diagnosis of and promising prescription for the church's infirmity. Those interested in the vitality of the church will be encouraged and instructed by the experiences and insights of James Harnish."

Kenneth L. Carder, Bishop, Mississippi Area, The United Methodist Church

"Jim Harnish has a strong and passionate heart for the gospel and for the ministry of local congregations. A leader in touch with the Great Physician, Harnish has written a powerful book that is just what the doctor ordered for those needing inspiration, wisdom, and the practices necessary for healthy, revitalized discipleship."

Gregory Jones, Dean, Duke University Divinity School

"This book is very accessible, down-to-earth, practical, and, most important, hopeful. It has its finger on the pulse of where church meets people, and this prescription for recovery, if followed, will help many pastors in serving their mainline churches."

James Howell, Senior Pastor, Myers Park UMC, Charlotte, North Carolina

"As is the case of Harnish's other books, this book is well written and engaging. I like the balance Harnish maintains in providing guidance to pastors and laity going through transformation. His advice on worship is a good example of the healthy balance he provides. I also like the thoroughness of Harnish's presentation. This will be a great resource for churches going through transformation or considering it."

Bishop Timothy Whitaker

"This is a terrific book written for me, the reader, from Harnish's heart and his experience with lots of appropriate illustrations."

Bishop Dick Wilke, The United Methodist Church

"The prescription for a healthy, vibrant, growing, mission-minded church is seemingly illogical: to live is to die. Yet this oxymoron is at the center of the gospel. Exhibiting the credibility that can come only from a practitioner, Jim Harnish has penned a classic for fellow preachers/pastors. His vulnerability and humility set the tone for ultimate truth. This book should be required reading every three years for every pastor in every denomination."

Timothy J. Bagwell, Director of New Congregational Development
South Georgia Conference, United Methodist Church

"Some people look at old city churches and ask despairingly, 'Can these elephants ever fly?' Jim Harnish and the people of Hyde Park are answering in the affirmative. Like others who are having the time of their lives helping old elephants fly, Jim and his people live the stories and then tell the stories of people meeting Jesus, people growing up as disciples, and people making God's grace known by living out servanthood. In a world of church revitalization books, this is a good read!"

Kent E. Kroehler, Sr., Pastor, First United Methodist Church, Lancaster, Pennsylvania

CPSIA information can be obtained at www.ICGtesting.com
Printed in the USA
LVOW06s0004271215

467788LV00009B/86/P